Moths & Caterpillars

of

Minnesota, Wisconsin & Michigan

Moths & Caterpillars *of* Minnesota, Wisconsin & Michigan

Jim Sogaard

Kollath+Stensaas
PUBLISHING

Kollath+Stensaas Publishing
394 Lake Avenue South, Suite 406
Duluth, MN 55802
Office: 218.727.1731
info@kollathstensaas.com
www.kollathstensaas.com
Orders: 800.678.7006
www.adventurewithkeen.com

MOTHS & CATERPILLARS
of MINNESOTA, WISCONSIN & MICHIGAN

[A revised & expanded edition of *Moths & Caterpillars of the North Woods*]

Printed in South Korea
10 9 8 7 6 5 4 3 2 1 First Printing

Editorial Director: Mark Sparky Stensaas
Graphic Designer: Rick Kollath

Illustrations by Rick Kollath, Kollath Graphic Design
Cover photos: Jim Sogaard [main, bottom right, bottom middle]
Sparky Stensaas [bottom left]

ISBN 978-1-936571-17-8

Table of Contents

Dedicated to

Mom,

who left us too soon

and loved the North Woods dearly

&

to the *Moths*,

long overlooked, misunderstood and undervalued

Acknowledgements

My parents gave me life, places to explore and five sisters who have endured me with good cheer.

W. J. Holland, Charles Covell, Jr. and Roger Tory Peterson provided excellent books on the moths of North America, tantalizing windows on their beauty and diversity. I have here especially relied upon Covell for wingspans and distribution ranges and upon David Wagner's book for caterpillar lengths.

The excellent work of Dan Janzen and Winnie Hallwachs has long fired my interest in biodiversity and ecology and provided a door to tropical exploration.

Three Rivers Parks District (formerly Hennepin County Parks) has allowed me to light-trap and photograph in their reserves through many seasons.

Les Ferge provided consultation on some of my identifications for which I am most grateful. Thanks to Chris Schmidt for helping with a out-of-range moth mystery, and also to David Wagner who aided in solving a caterpillar mystery. All final responsibility for identifications is of course mine.

Ron and Cathy Huber have provided guidance and encouragement.

Les Ferge and George Balogh published a Wisconsin moth checklist that greatly expanded my view of our regional fauna and upon which I have relied heavily for seasonal and distributional records.

Nancy Haugen has offered encouragement and use of her home and woods through many seasons of light trapping, caterpillar rearing and photography.

I thank my publishers at Kollath-Stensaas for their interest and support. I especially acknowledge the effort invested in scanning my film-captured images. I had neither a scanner nor the skills and they took a load off my shoulders.

Jim Sogaard
June 11, 2009

The Publishers are grateful to Clinton Dexter-Nienhaus for reviewing the text revisions and layout. Kyle Johnson provided a quick last-minute review of identifications. Thank you both!

May 20, 2025

Introduction

Minnesota, Wisconsin and Michigan each have about 2,500 (not mutually exclusive) species of Lepidoptera and Ontario, likely as many. Distributions in place and time and details of ecology, are poorly known for most species. Some species are widespread and common, others local, uncommon or rare, but it is harder to assess rarity or spotty distribution. While there are truly rare species, rarity is sometimes only apparent, due to inadequate sampling and may merit doubt. Sometimes scarce species become common for a season or more and common species can become scarce for one or more seasons, sometimes permanently. Some moths cannot survive winter this far north and re-colonize each year, others stray here very rarely. Global climate change will likely affect flight seasons, distribution ranges, winter survival, seasonality and distribution of caterpillar and adult food plants, parasites and diseases and every aspect of the biology.

Most moth species have broad distributions. No exclusively local (endemic) species are known for our region. The Io Moth occurs not only in boreal forests of the North Woods, but also in North Dakota and Costa Rica. Moths of boreal forests often range very widely in northern latitudes, even around the globe. Recent DNA analyses have shown some moths to be two or more closely related "cryptic" species and more such will surely be found.

Such large group poses many challenges, compounded by constraints of field-guide portability. I have "cherry-picked" to fire interest, but have balanced this "celebrity" focus with genus, family and ecological group introductions for a wider perspective. If you do not find your moth or caterpillar here, take a photo or a specimen and look into the online and book resources listed in the back of this guide.

There are about 12,400 species of Lepidoptera named in North America. Of these about 830—only 7 percent—are butterflies. While moths are somewhat inconvenient due to their nocturnal habits, they are amazingly diverse, often fascinating and sometimes dazzling. Attentiveness will yield rich rewards.

A portable field guide can hold only so much. This one introduces 372 species of the over 3,000 in Minnesota, Wisconsin and Michigan. I believe this is a good start. I hope it brings you much pleasure of discovery!

Moths in the Biosphere

Much overlooked, moths are abundant, diverse and ecologically important. With over 180,000 known species world-wide, hundreds are still being described each year. Adults range from mosquito- to bird-sized, may be wingless or migratory, live hours to months. The feeding caterpillar stage may last a week or over a decade.

Moths influence ecology in many ways. Caterpillars are the largest natural consumers of vegetation, outstripping ants, termites, elephants and deer. At outbreak levels Forest Tent Caterpillars can reach a biomass equivalent to about 1,800 caribou per square mile, hunted by 220 wolves-worth of tachinid fly parasitoids (Jens Roland, University of Alberta). Feeding adults pollinate many plants, from trees to orchids, sometimes in very specialized relationships. Moths, in all their life stages, are important food for spiders, insects, birds, lizards, frogs, fish, rodents, bats, bears, armadillos, monkeys and shrews. As hosts to specialized parasitoid wasps and flies, moths support a huge part of insect biodiversity while contributing greatly to their own control. As plant parasites and predators caterpillars greatly influence forest health, bird reproduction and nutrient cycling in terrestrial and aquatic ecosystems (as part of the food web, as sources of nutrient release and as recyclers of dead vegetation). Many things of value, such as caffeine, chocolate, spices and medicines have arisen as plant responses to insects (and other creatures) eating them. A tiny part of the moth fauna competes importantly with us for wood, fruits, nuts, vegetables, grains, carpets and clothing. The little Indian Meal Moth is the number one pest infesting stored foods worldwide. The Meal Moth, another cosmopolitan associate of humans that attacks stored foods, can carry rat tapeworm eggs able to infest humans. During outbreaks some moths and caterpillars can cause significant public health problems such as asthma, allergy and dermatitis by way of airborne setae (scales). Some moths that feed on the blood, sweat or tears of mammals and birds are suspected of carrying eye diseases. Some tropical caterpillars are nearly as feared as venomous snakes for their painful stings and livestock can die from accidentally eating them.

What are Moths?

Our misperception of moths is remarkable. Though they make up the great majority of Lepidoptera, they are eclipsed (in our minds) by one small derivative branch, the butterflies. This is like mistaking movie stars for humanity and humans for ghosts; quite a tail-wagging-the-dog story! Essentially, all Lepidoptera are moths. The difference between moths and butterflies (including skippers) is minor. Butterflies are a small recent offshoot of colorful, visual, day-active moths that perhaps "fled" into cover of daylight from predatory bats and/or colonized the daytime to exploit day-flowering plants. Recognizing this in no way diminishes butterflies, but enriches them with context. Lepidoptera arose in the Jurassic Period (about 190 million years ago) when dinosaurs reigned and greatly expanded in diversity, along with the flowering plants, during the Cretaceous (late dinosaurs) and Tertiary (mammals). Much of the rapid expansion of diversity is very recent, making interpretation of the family tree more difficult, but the basal ancestry is much clearer. Lepidoptera is the most recently arisen insect order, sharing closest ancestry with the caddisflies (Order Trichoptera). Ideally our classification will come to reflect ancestry, but we are not very close yet.

The Order Lepidoptera contains many more than the 180,000 so-far-described species worldwide and over 12,400 species in North America. Lepidoptera comes from the Greek *lepido* (scale) and *ptera* (wing). The scales are specialized bristles (setae) arranged like overlapping shingles on a roof. Various setae also occur on the body and appendages of adults, on caterpillars and on some pupae. When we call moths or caterpillars "hairy," we mean they have hair-like setae, not the hair of mammals.

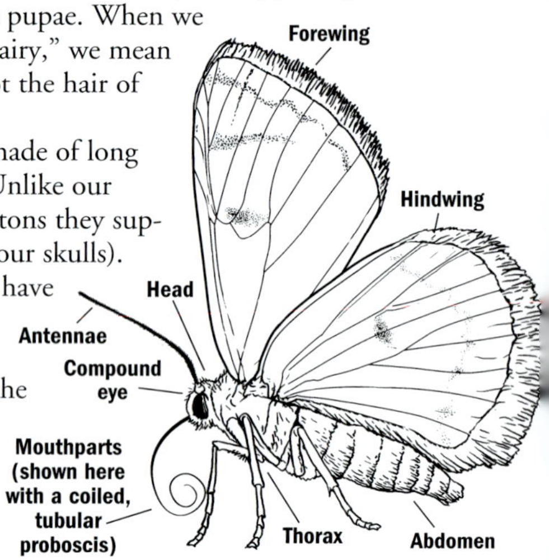

Insect exoskeletons are made of long sugar chains called chitin. Unlike our bony, mostly internal, skeletons they support from the outside (like our skulls). Ironically, insect heads also have an internal skeleton—internal extensions of the head capsule, that support the "sucking pump" and its muscles and muscles for head movement. The insect head represents the fusion of probably six ancestral segments, with appendages such as the proboscis, antennae and labial palps, being highly modified derivatives of ancestral legs.

Adult Moths

Adult moths have three body sections: a head, with a compound eye on each side, most often with a (sometimes obscure) simple eye (ocellus) near its top edge, two sensory antennae and various mouthparts, including a tubular proboscis, usually held coiled (a few very primitive moths have chewing mouthparts); a thorax with three segments, each bearing a pair of true legs and the hind two each (usually) bearing a pair of wings; and an abdomen of ten segments, the hindmost two highly modified into reproductive structures.

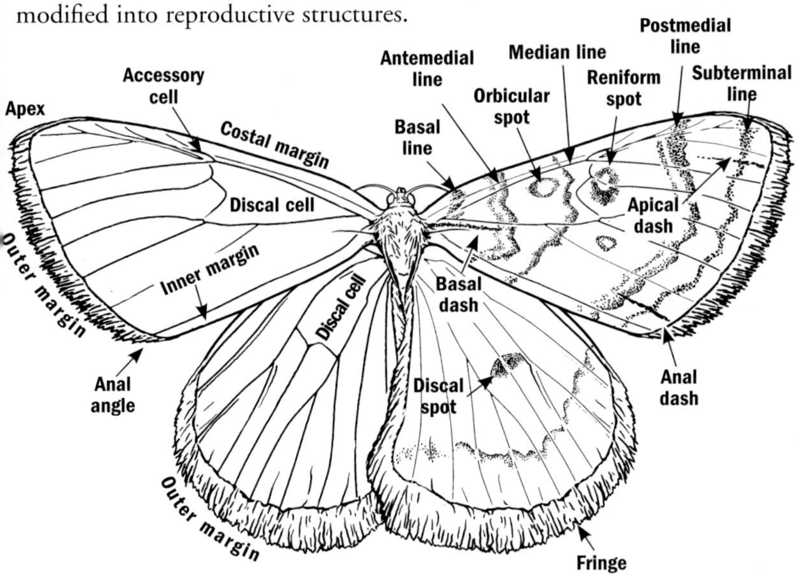

Caterpillars

Caterpillars have a head with six simple eyes on each side, sensory antennae (much smaller than in adults) and various chewing mouthparts; three thoracic segments, each bearing a pair of true legs and ten abdominal segments, bearing a total of two to five pairs of fleshy, unjointed, gripping prolegs.

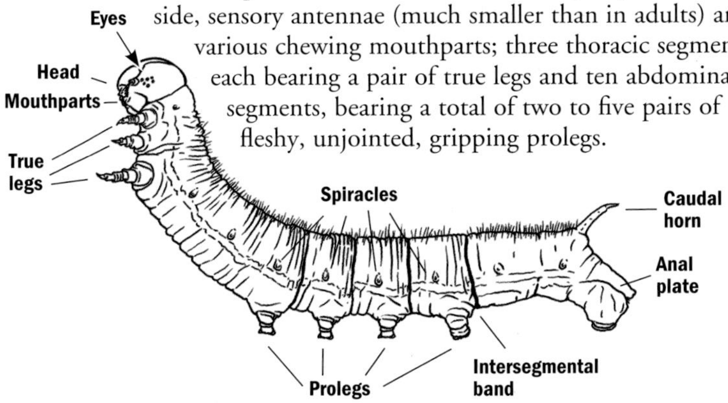

Beware the Imposters!

Other insect larvae can be confused with caterpillars. Sawflies are wasps whose larvae are variously caterpillar-like. They are easily told apart by a single simple eye on each side of the head, rather than six and by having more than the two to five pairs of prolegs present in all but very few caterpillars. Hoverfly larvae look and crawl like leeches, alternately hunching up and stretching out. They have a close-set pair of stalked spiracles at the rear and feed on aphids. Some beetle larvae could be confused with caterpillars, but they lack prolegs.

This is the larva of the Elm Sawfly (*Cimbex americana*).

***Nematus* sawfly larvae also feed like moth caterpillars.**

Syrphid fly larva could be mistaken for a caterpillar.

Moth Biology & Behavior

Moths are among the nine-tenths of living insect species with complete metamorphosis in four stages: egg, larva (caterpillar), pupa and adult. The stages have basic roles but some needs (e.g. wintering) are variously met in different species. Eggs are nurseries for early cell growth and differentiation. Their shells keep moisture in and microorganisms and UV radiation out. Caterpillars gather resources, especially energy and nitrogen, being basically guts with jaws. Pupae are changing rooms where all but a few islands of caterpillar cells "dissolve" and reorganize into adults in a radically different selective expression of the same set of genes. Adults connect; males (usually) fly to find mates guided by airborne chemical (pheromone) signals released by females. Females fly to place fertilized eggs on plants suited to the survival and nourishment of the caterpillars. The search for caterpillar food is guided by airborne and surface plant chemicals and sometimes by vision. Adult flight is the main means of spatial dispersal, for genetic mixing and resource location.

Moths can be large and beautiful like this Twin-spotted Sphinx...or tiny and drab. They comprise 95 percent of all Lepidoptera.

Parasitoids and other Enemies

Parasitoids, especially various families of wasps and tachinid flies, are a large array of specialized predators that take a great toll (likely the single greatest mortality factor) on many invertebrates, including moths and butterflies. Despite the name, they nearly always behave more like predators, killing their prey, than like parasites, which usually do not. Eggs, caterpillars and pupae are all vulnerable. Adults can be infested by mites that attach and suck hemolymph or live in their ears, or by roundworms that feed in the digestive tract, but these better qualify as parasites.

This unfortunate *Hypena deceptalis* caterpillar is carrying around its death sentence in the form of green brachonid wasp larvae.

Parasitoids are extremely diverse. They range from tiny to quite large. Some attack many host species, others only one. They variously inject their eggs into their victims, glue them to the surface or lay them near caterpillars which eat them and are attacked from within. Some are hyperparasitoids, preying on other parasitoids already inside a host. Some parasitoid larvae pupate within the cadaver, some exit and pupate in the soil, and others form cocoons on the surface of the victim. Parasitoids largely depend on volatile chemicals released by damaged leaves, silk, frass and cuticle (especially at molt) to find their hosts.

Developing wasps have eaten the insides of the caterpillar host and pupatied on the outside of their victim.

Parasitoids appear to prefer chemically defended hosts, because the host defenses also protect the parasitoid from being eaten by a predator.

Parasitoids are of great importance in controlling insect numbers and the damage they do to vegetation. Strong evidence suggests that parasitoid presence has been declining, likely because increasing climatic variability is making it harder for them to track their hosts through time.

Other organisms also take a toll on Lepidoptera. Prominent among these are predatory ants and wasps, beetles and spiders. Viruses, bacteria and a variety of fungi also play minor to major roles in Lepidoptera mortality, sometimes building up during outbreaks and leading to population crashes.

It's not always other insects. Fungus has done in this now unrecognizable caterpillar.

Behavioral options increase with mobility, but even the least mobile stages can surprise. Eggs of at least one species are dispersed by birds, traveling undamaged through their digestion after egg-laden females drop to the ground and are eaten. Some pupae can flex to catch small predators in sharp-edged creases (known as gin-trapping), or startle predators by thrashing about or resembling a snake, orient to light for seasonal cues, or move to the surface to eclose by abdominal telescoping.

Avoiding being noticed is a primary defense of adult moths; and matching the color and background of your perch is a good way to accomplish this.

Staying Alive

Staying alive to complete basic tasks is the other main job in all stages. Camouflage (crypsis), masquerade, startle and warning (aposematism) are the main ways to avoid or deflect predators.

Camouflage (crypsis)

Primary defense avoids notice and secondary defense avoids being eaten once discovered. A great part of adult moth behavior, often called resting, is really hiding. The regular postures of moths, standard for each species, as often resemble yoga poses as "resting" reposes. To describe such moth as resting robs it of behavior; better to say it is "perching." The fact that moths hold their bodies in ways that combine profiles and textures with colors, shadings and markings to create remarkable camouflage, masquerade or warning, argues against so bland a term as "resting;" pinned specimens rest in a drawer, live moths perch. Live, motionless, moths are not always perched. A moth come recently to rest at a light is often better described as "at rest" than perched. Captured moths seek escape by flying, running or dropping

Camouflage—matching the substrate...

...wing reticulations match the decay pattern of a skeletonized leaf.

...mottled greens of the wings blend with tree trunk lichens.

...just another fallen leaf on the forest floor.

...profile obscured by markings —Where does the twig end and the moth begin?

and "playing dead." Once at rest they may suddenly or gradually perch. Going to perch often involves rhythmic rocking of the body and shallow pumping of wings, suggesting the moth is fitting itself into place and into itself, obscuring shadows and profiles, antennae folded back under the wings, the face tucked between the extended hairy forelegs.

Besides posture, perching involves particular orientations and settings, such as the underside of a live leaf, or along the axis of a twig, or sideways or head-down on tree bark or head pressed to the surface of leaves on the forest floor. Some moths scurry under leaf litter or into dark nooks to hide. Whether such cover seekers assume rigorous perching postures is a good question, but seems less likely.

Once perched, a moth may remain motionless for hours, except perhaps to adjust its position relative to changing light, for reasons of crypsis or thermoregulation. It is in this "pretending not to be a moth" that moths best show their understated charisma. Pinned specimens have many good uses, but for sheer strange beauty and entertainment, live, perched moths are far superior. (No one goes bird watching in a museum.)

Moth Masquerades

In cases of masquerade or warning, moths or caterpillars are not hiding, but advertising. Some look like bird droppings and perch in full view, very conspicuously atop leaves, as if shouting "I'm worthless, ignore me." This is not mimicry since the resemblance is to something, such as a bird dropping, twig or leaf, not of interest to the signal receiver (especially, a hungry bird). Unlike camouflage, masquerade does not depend on matching a background. Resemblance to dead leaves is a particularly common presentation in adult moths. Dead leaves being so common, this makes sense. Whether a dead-leaf moth is matching a background of dead leaves (i.e. is cryptic) or is masquerading as a leaf is a good question. I suspect both occur. A similar situation pertains to twig-like caterpillars.

Masquerade—resembling something inedible...

...a broken twig.

...a bird dropping, complete with splotchiness.

...a piece of curled bark.

...a drooping leaf.

Startle displays

Startle displays involve sudden changes in appearance, often involving flashing of brightly colored, boldly patterned hindwings. Startle may scare off a predator or gain a split-second head-start toward escape.

Scaring to survive

Owl-like false eyes may make a predator do an about-face.

This moth can emit toxic yellow froth and produce squeaking sounds.

Bright hind wings flash upon take-off when alarmed.

False eyes could direct an attack at the hind wings instead of the vulnerable body.

Other moth survival strategies

This day-flying moth likely advertises its inedibility with bright colors.

Sheer size and speed may protect this sphinx moth.

This moth is a very convincing mimic of a wasp. Predators may stay away.

A predator would think twice as bright colors often means the moth is chemically defended. It also has a very colorful abdomen that may startle would-be predators.

Eggs

Moth eggs vary greatly, from thin and tightly pressed to the surface, to spherical, hemispherical or columnar. Their surfaces may be smooth or intricately sculpted. They may be dispersed singly or in small clusters or laid in large single-layer patches or multi-layered clumps or strewn broadly from flight. Size varies greatly. They often change color soon after laying or as hatching nears. Egg laying females often avoid plants already bearing eggs of their own species, cued visually or chemically. The shells are sometimes the first meal of newly hatched caterpillars.

Spongy Moth (*Lymantria dispar*) female with her recently lain eggs.

Caterpillars

Moths that winter as eggs have great pressure to synchronize hatching with leafing out of their food plants. Such caterpillars need tender young leaves (or flowers) to survive. Since bud-break is variable between individual plants and between years, this challenge is partly met by the ability of the youngest caterpillars to extrude silk strands from their salivary glands and ride them downwind, sometimes repeatedly, until they find nutrition or perish. A season or more with especially good synchrony of hatching with leafing may produce outbreaks in some species. Moth caterpillars are highly diverse in size, shape, color, patterning, texture, hairiness, diet, defenses and behaviors. Beyond feeding, in species with flightless females, caterpillars drifting on silk contribute to dispersal and caterpillars are often involved in winter diapause. In most species there are usually five or six larval stages (instars) between molts, but this can vary with food supply. When a growing caterpillar exceeds the "fit" of its cuticle (skin), stretch receptors trigger molting hormones. The caterpillar quits feeding and grows a new cuticle inside the old one before splitting it and crawling out. Shed cuticle is often eaten to retain nutrients or defensive chemicals.

Caterpillars often eat living leaves, but also, variously, flowers, fruits, seeds, stems, roots, dead leaves, dung, wood, wax, skin, horn, fur, feathers, fungi, algae, lichens, mosses, liverworts, stored food products, wool sweaters and carpets, other caterpillars or pupae, other insect eggs, larvae, nymphs or adults, snails and earthworms. Some are aquatic and have gills, swimming ashore to pupate. Larvae of Planthopper Parasite Moths (Epipyropidae) attach to their hosts and feed on their waxy secretions.

Caterpillars must "bring home the bacon" despite predators, parasitoids, pathogens, physical stressors (wind, aridity, heat, cold) and

Caterpillar Camouflage (crypsis)

...blemished leaf, brown spots and all.

...flower parts.

...fruit pod of host plant.

...rough edge of a toothed leaf.

...conifer needles.

Caterpillar Masquerades (resembling something inedible)

...twig with bud scars.

...tattered leaf or catkin.

...bird droppings.

...bird droppings.

...fallen dead leaf.

Other Caterpillar Survival Strategies

Glands just behind the head, are able to squirt formic and acetic acid several inches in a somewhat controlled direction.

Size may discourage some but this caterpillar can also make snapping or rasping sounds by rubbing their mandibles together.

When disturbed this caterpillar extrudes bright red filaments which emit a volatile chemical.

Venomous spines are a discouragement to many.

Which is the head? Confusion may deflect attacks away from true head.

Group feeding helps magnify warning signs.

a considerable array of plant defenses, including elusiveness in place and time, physical toughness, stinging spines, chemical recruitment of predators and parasitoids, housing and feeding resident body guards (especially ants), induced chemical defenses, signaling impending attack to neighboring plants, chemical interference with digestion, poisoning the caterpillar or keeping it from maturing through hormonal manipulation. Contrary to popular belief, a vegetarian diet is often not bland or benign. Plants are loaded with defensive chemicals. It is usually not entirely clear why they came to be—whether the tannin that interferes with caterpillar digestion today came about to that end or earlier, to deter a fungus or bacterium, or earlier still to serve some non-defensive role in the plant.

Caterpillars have an impressive array of counter-responses. The least acidic naturally-occurring environment known on Earth is the mid-gut of caterpillars, which markedly disarms some defensive plant chemistry (such as the ability of tannins to tie-up proteins), as

Some caterpillars will kill and eat caterpillars of other moth and butterfly species. [*Lithophane* species]

Hairiness may discourage some insects and some birds.

A large "eye" may make a bird or other predator think twice.

Bright colors may mean this caterpillar is chemically defended (i.e. tastes bad).

Feeding on the undersides of leaves helps this slug caterpillar hide from birds.

do the membranes surrounding their digestive tracts and their very active enzymatic detoxification systems. Caterpillars often feed in ways that disarm their food plants, such as mowing off stinging hairs or severing pressurized latex channels.

Some caterpillars in harsh climates or with low-nutrient diets need more than one year to mature. Tussock moths (Lymantriidae) in the genus *Gynaephora* living in severe arctic and alpine environments need ten or more years to complete development, feeding on dwarf shrubs. Many carpenterworm moths (Cossidae) feeding on wood, which is very low in nitrogen, need two or more years. Wood-rotting fungi often trap bacteria or roundworms to supplement their nitrogen and one might ask how important "carnivory" is to wood-eating caterpillars. Cannibalism is known in wood-eating ghost moth caterpillars.

Because swift evasion (as in leaping from a perch or bungee-dropping on a silk thread) is limited and risky (losing the host plant, blundering into predators) most caterpillars use other defenses such as: feeding inside their food, resembling their own feeding damage, spinning solitary or communal silk shelters, bearing stiff or luxuriant, "hair" barriers or venomous spines, exuding sticky repellents, flashing threatening signals (false eyes, snake heads, warning colors), squirting streams of acid, whipping about eversible tentacles that dispense volatile

The enormous size of some sphinx moths, as well as their ability to move rapidly from side to side while hovering, may have evolved to deal with predators.

chemicals, thrashing, biting, squeaking or clicking loudly, regurgitating gut contents, throwing frass to avoid detection by parasitoids, sensing the flight sounds of approaching parasitoids, gathering and storing toxins from food plants, synthesizing toxins, removing partly-eaten leaves to reduce visual and chemical evidence, leaving or relocating on the food plant, perching so as to increase harvesting cost to predators, burrowing into the soil or litter or hiding in bark crevices when not feeding, feeding only at night, hiding by matching the general background, or by masquerading as something inedible to predators such as a leaf or stem or dung. Some predators are avoided by being too small to be worth the effort of harvesting, or too big to conveniently or safely harvest.

Defenses are always conditional, more or less effective against different predators and parasites (Gentry and Dyer, 2002). Size will draw some predators while foiling others. Hairiness may deter ants and bugs, but not wasps. Bright coloration may repel wasps but have little effect on ants and bugs. While solitary, dispersed, exposed feeding is effective against flies, living as a group in a silk-tied shelter is dangerous exposure to parasitoid flies because of all the concentrated odor cues (silk, frass, cuticle, feeding damage). Yet there are clearly cases where it makes sense all the same. Wasps are best deterred by biting, dropping and regurgitating. Ironically, chemical defense against vertebrate predators often makes caterpillars more desirable hosts for parasitoids, since the chemical defending the caterpillar also protects the parasitoids within from being incidentally eaten. Against parasitoids, the foremost agents of doom (Cornell and Hawkins, 1995), defense by regurgitation and solitary living (which makes them harder to find) may be as good as it gets.

Transitions

When sufficient resources are acquired, caterpillars quit feeding and, now known as prepupae, often dramatically change color, sometimes shrinking and looking sickly, often crawling restlessly in search of a pupation site. Some simply void their guts and drop to the ground where they spin a cocoon or pupate unprotected in the leaf litter. Only a few species form elaborate silk cocoons on plants. Many need a particular type and depth of soil, or soft dead wood, in which to burrow and form a "cell" with sides compacted, lined or sealed with silk. Many species winter as pupae, others as prepupae, pupating in spring, or as pharate adults inside the pupal case. Not uncommonly, some portion of the offspring remains in diapause for more than one winter—sometimes for several or more, until more favorable cues are received. This insures against any one inhospitable season wiping out most or all of a population. Control of diapause is probably most often facultative (environmentally cued), but can be genetically hard-wired. In some populations of the Cecropia Moth in the Midwest, all matings produce offspring programmed to eclose early and late in a given season, to spread risk against the vagaries of a given spring. These are clearly two kinds of flexibility with the same benefit. The documented record for extended diapause survival, under manipulated laboratory conditions is apparently 30 years (Powell, 2001)

The cocoon of the Spotted Tussock Moth includes many larval hairs felted together with silk.

Silk cocoon of the Promethea Moth.

Eclosion

Despite variables of genetics and microclimatic differences between diapause sites, adults are able to eclose (emerge) in remarkable synchrony. This is especially critical in species whose adults cannot feed and have very short life spans. Males often eclose a day or so before females.

Love is in the air...literally!

Females usually do not fly before mating. They climb vegetation and, at a programmed, light-cued hour, fan their wings and release volatile chemical mating lures to which males are acutely sensitive. Males, also on a genetic clock and cued to light levels through the ocelli, take flight, sifting the air with their antennae. When the mating scent is detected a sequence of flight patterns ensues by which the male homes in on the "calling" female. Some males, once near the female, also emit chemical signals, from large, elaborate, eversible structures called coremata or from specialized tufts of scales on the wings, legs or abdomen. Some males also, or alternatively, produce ultrasonic signals just before mating. Actual mating may be brief or take many hours.

In the following nights males may fly in search of further mates. Females less often mate again (see below) flying only to place fertilized eggs on or near appropriate food plants over one or more nights. In some species females are unable to fly, so do not disperse the eggs, but rather place them on or very near the plant upon which they themselves fed as a caterpillar or even on the cocoon from which they eclosed. Flightlessness lets females invest more into producing eggs (rather than flight equipment and fuel) and avoids the predation risk of flying.

Variations on mating are many. In some ghost moths and in saltmarsh tiger moths, males are the primary chemical signalers, either while stationary or while flying.

Often males contribute not only genes and the energy and risk of spatial connection but also carbohydrates, scarce minerals, and/or defensive chemicals. Sometimes mating "packets" keep females from mating again, protecting paternal investment. In other cases male-gathered resources are the incentive for multiple mating by females, without donor males gaining paternal benefit.

Longevity is a relative term

Some adults (e.g. giant silk moths) live about a week, others (such as female tent caterpillar moths) may mate, lay eggs and die in a day. Hawk moths, most able to feed as adults, can live for months. Male and female giant silk moths differ more or less markedly since males are specialized to find females and females are specialized to distribute heavy egg loads to appropriate food plants. Male and female hawk moths differ less as they share a need to fly in search of nectar and water to stay alive long enough to maximize reproduction.

Going batty

The influence of and interaction with predatory bats is a major area of ecological study in Lepidoptera. Bats may have produced butterflies and surely gave rise to hearing in many flying insects (six or seven times in Lepidoptera) and to tiger moths' ability to produce their own ultrasonic calls, likely to advertise their chemical defense. Hearing allows moths to detect and avoid hunting bats by erratic flight, diving, or dropping. Moths without hearing rely on other means to reduce their vulnerability, such as flying when bats are not a-wing (early or late season, diurnally), flying less or lower to the ground or being very large or very fast. But, there are no sure answers. Some bats are unusually quiet and hard to detect or able to find and capture perched moths and caterpillars.

The larval advantage

The widespread occurrence of complete metamorphosis, defined by a larval stage, raises the question of its advantage. Possibly greater feeding efficiency reduces the need for adult feeding. The efficiency gain may largely owe to a much lower investment of nitrogen and carbohydrate in cuticle (in caterpillars only one-tenth that of grasshopper nymphs). Insects with complete metamorphosis also have shorter life-cycles which may reduce exposure to parasitoids and other predators. Or perhaps having a larval stage makes the life cycle more flexibly responsive to environmental demands.

Moth Appreciation & Study

Other sources being available on this topic, I'll be selective and brief. Observe what comes to lights or is perched where lights were lit the night before and what is around you in gardens, yards and parks. It is amazing how much we walk past unawares. If you slow down to look very carefully, you will see much more. It can be a very challenging and engaging game of hide and seek. If you wish to go further, there are many ways: placing light traps, sugar bait and pheromone traps to capture adult moths; using a sweep net, beating tray and headlamp for day and night-time caterpillar searches; using photography to document encounters, life stages, variability and behaviors; rearing caterpillars found in nature or obtained from eggs laid by captured females for caterpillar identifications, photos, parasitoids and fresh adults; making a properly labeled reference collection as a learning tool and to document occurrences and variations; winter searching for cocoons; studying the literature and web-sites; and sharing your collection, records and photos to expand and share knowledge.

Key jingling

You can trigger bat-evasion behaviors by jingling a ring of keys near flying moths. The key-jingling sound contains ultrasound which can cause dropping, diving or spiraling flight in moths with ears. Bat detectors can make the ultrasonic calls of bats and moths audible.

Turn it on and they will come

The easiest way to find moths is to search near existing lights or set up a light trap. A white sheet placed behind or under the light makes the moths much easier to see. Moths are not so much attracted to light as trapped by it, though no one knows exactly how. [The Navaho thought moths insane (since their lights were fires). Others took moths for the wandering souls of the dead, ever in search of light.] Given light pollution and eroding biodiversity, use lights carefully, insofar as how much (even a 6 or 12 watt black-light powered by D-cells or a motorcycle battery can be very productive), where, for how long, how many specimens you collect and how well you label, use and share your collection. The impact of collecting is usually trivial, but mindful conservatism is best. Some dislike the very idea of collecting, but most people have cars with "collections" on their radiator grills that contribute nothing to learning, education or conservation. Collections are only as good as their data (place, date, collector's name and means of acquisition) and need protection from pests such as carpet beetles and mold.

A method to occasionally attract a few moths for you and your family to enjoy and identify is to simply keep an outside house or garage light on all night. But get out early in the morning while the moths are still cool and sluggish. Once warmed up, most will take flight. But use this method only occasionally as the resident birds, frogs, and squirrels will quickly catch on and devour the night's selection. If you want a nicer background for photographing the moths, place a flattened piece of bark on the wall near the light.

A simple light trap at night can attract a wide variety of moths and other insects.

Rearing your own

You can photograph captured moths, obtain eggs from which to rear caterpillars and obtain fresh adults for photography, voucher specimens to document records of occurrence, analysis of adult variation, etc. Rearing can be highly productive but must not be undertaken casually. Captive adults and caterpillars need careful tending (air; fresh appropriate food; climate control, etc.). Collected or reared adults should be documented, labeled, shared and ultimately, submitted to research collections. Live animals should never be released outside their usual range, where they might cause problems. Releases should be made as near the place (and time) of origin as possible. Reared moths often eclose out of synch with wild populations and collecting a specimen often makes more sense than release.

Once in a while you may want to leave a porch or garage light on to attract a few moths. Tacking flat pieces of bark near the lights can provide a better background for photography.

The inside scoop

In some translucent caterpillars internal anatomy can be viewed. The pulse is visible as a series of rapid, rhythmic waves passing forward in the dorsal midline. The tracheal network, branching out intricately from the spiracles, can sometimes be seen waving, suspended, in the hemolymph. The paired, pale, testes of male caterpillars are sometimes visible subdorsally at about the fifth abdominal segment.

UV is groovy

Flourescence can be your friend when trying to find moth larvae at night. Many caterpillars contain pigments that absorb UV light and

then re-emit it as visible light, causing them to glow. And quite a few caterpillar species are active at night, making UV flashlight surveys a valuable tool for studying their behavior and ecology. This method can be used to find caterpillars of all instars, make finding them easier, and provide insights into an area's biodiversity. UV/Blacklight flashlights can be bought online, but note that some naturalists get better results with UV light in the 365 nanometer (nm) wavelength versus the 385-395nm range.

How to use this Field Guide

Moths and Caterpillars of Minnesota, Wisconsin & Michigan is designed to make field identification easier for you, the reader. Through the use of color photos of both moths and caterpillars, wingspan bars, gender symbols, phenograms and caterpillar food plants, we have made a handy, compact and easy to use guide. It is small enough to tuck into any daypack.

Coverage

We have made no attempt to include all the species of the three state's moth fauna. Instead, we have highlighted the most common, several of the bizarre, a few of the most colorful moths. We have concentrated on the "macroleps," which tend to be larger and showier than the "microleps." Herein, moths from 11 families of macrolepidoptera and a small sampling of ten families of microlepidoptera are treated.

Not all species are found in any single area. Larval food plant preferences may limit some species to habitats where that tree, bush or flower may grow. Distributions in place and time and details of ecology, are poorly known for most species. Some species are widespread and common, others local, uncommon or rare, but it is harder to assess rarity or spotty distribution. While there are truly rare species, rarity is sometimes only apparent, due to inadequate sampling and may merit doubt.

Names

Scientific and common names are given for all species. The most widely accepted common name from online published sources such as the Moth Photographers Group and iNaturalist were used.

Phenograms

Flight seasons are shown in the red-bar phenogram below the adult photo. Real season-to-season and place-to-place flight periods are often much more limited. It is worth noting that some species (especially some northern noctuids, sesiids, etc.) regularly fly mostly in odd or even years likely as a way of avoiding parasitoids.

Range

Brief descriptions describe North American distribution based on dot maps from iNaturalist and the Moth Photographers Group. Ranges will become more detailed as community observations increase.

Nature Notes

Unless specified, assume the moths included in this guide come to lights. But be aware that some do so only after midnight when even many moth seekers turn off the lights and turn in. These are best sampled by all-night light traps not requiring attendance. I have made note of species that seem resistant or immune to light trapping.

Caterpillar descriptions

Descriptions apply to the final stage unless otherwise noted.

Size bars

Median wingspan is represented by the size bar. In a very few species who show great sexual dimorphism we have included a size bar for both sexes. Caterpillar size bars represent average final instar lengths.

MPG Numbers

We have chosen to use numbers assigned by the online Moth Photographers Group. The 2-number prefix represents the superfamily.

Sun icon

Day-flying moths are denoted by a small sun icon. This does not, in all cases, mean that they do not also fly at night. In some species it is only the male that flies during the day; in these cases we have placed a small male symbol inside the sun.

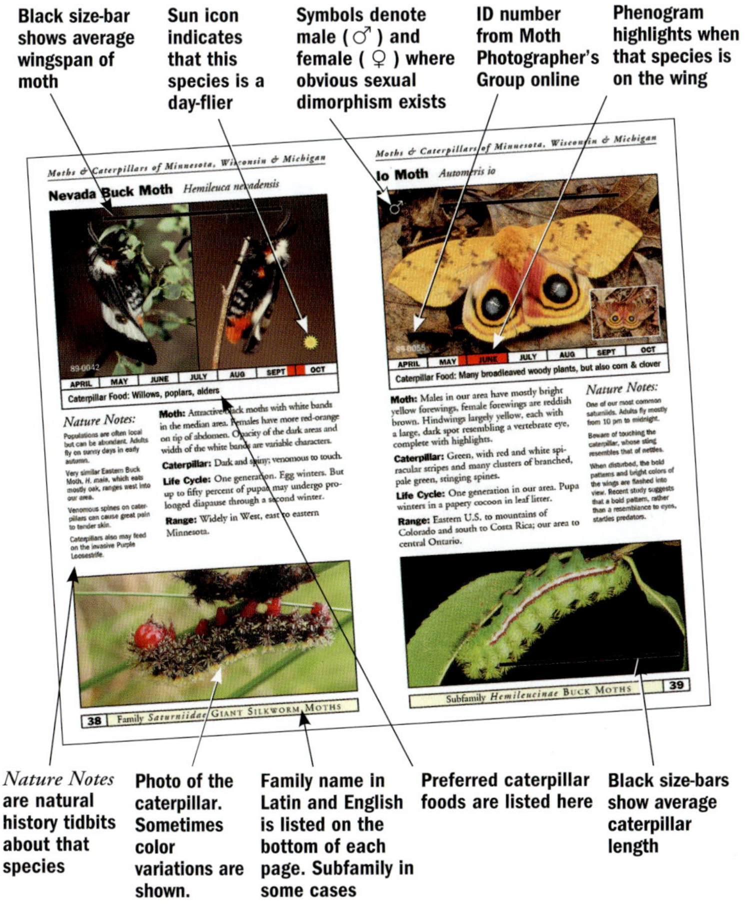

Macrolepidoptera

Description

Macrolepidoptera (Higher Ditrysia) is a somewhat arbitrary grouping of convenience, including the larger moths and the butterflies. Ditrysia, defined by separate openings for mating and laying eggs, is monophyletic and comprises about 95 percent of living Lepidoptera.

Two "macrolep" families have not been included in this guide due to having few members in our region. Sack-bearer Moths (Mimallonidae) are about 200 medium-sized moths, mostly in the American tropics. The common name refers to silk-tied leaf cases in which later-stage caterpillars feed and winter and (our species) pupate. Silkworm and Apatelodine Moths (Bombycidae) was a mostly Old World tropical family of around 60 species, recently enlarged by combination with about 250 species of mostly neotropical moths formerly placed in the now defunct family Apatelodidae.

Hooktip & False Owlet Moths Family Drepanidae

Description

Drepanidae has recently been enlarged to include the former family Thyatiridae based on similarity of the thoracic ears, with the tympanal membrane uniquely located between two enlarged interior tracheal chambers, rather than exposed externally.

Most larval and adult stages are cryptic, resembling dead leaves. *Eudeilinea* is somewhat odd; the adults are bright white, perhaps warning of chemical defense. The proboscis varies widely between species but it is present and presumably used in most of our species.

Caterpillars

Caterpillars in the subfamily Depraninae lack functional hind prolegs, these fused into a tail-like structure or a tubercle. Some caterpillars transmit sound signals as part of their territorial defense of feeding shelters. Caterpillars are able to toss their frass some distance, likely to reduce odor cues used by parasitoids to locate their prey.

Diversity (Species Richness/Range)

There are over 1000 species described worldwide, with greatest diversity in the Old-World tropics. North America has 20 species, including eight in our region.

Lettered Habrosyne *Habrosyne scripta*

APRIL	MAY	JUNE	JULY	AUG	SEPT	OCT

Caterpillar Food: Birches, blackberries, raspberries

Moth: Forewings are gray-brown with white costal, antemedial and postmedial areas accented with pink. White antemedial line bordering the brown basal patch gently angled.

Caterpillar: Orange-brown, with fine mottling and thin dark mid-dorsal line. Head more orange, with much reticulation. Perhaps indistinguishable from those of the *Pseudothyatira*.

Life Cycle: One generation in our region. Pupa winters.

Range: Northeastern U.S. to Pacific Northwest; Newfoundland to British Columbia.

Nature Notes:

Usually uncommon, but many adults once came to my light in northeastern Minnesota. Such an experience can distort expectations of usual abundance.

Adults have been seen at sugar bait.

There are just two North American *Habrosyne* species and others in the Old World.

Dogwood Thyatirid *Euthyatira pudens*

APRIL	MAY	JUNE	JULY	AUG	SEPT	OCT

Caterpillar Food: Dogwoods

Nature Notes:

Caterpillars resemble chemically defended sawfly larvae (order Hymenoptera) in their smooth, waxy surface, large dark spots on their heads and contrasting body coloration.

Adults perch with their wings wrapped around a twig, resembling mottled dead leaves.

Adults sometimes come to sugar bait.

Moth: Forewing gray, with large pinkish white patches at base, midpoint of costa and apex. A less common form, "*pennsylvanica,*" is gray overall, with a black apical dash.

Caterpillar: Smooth and waxy, pale to dark gray above the orange spiracles and whitish below. Head white, heavily mottled, with a large black spot at top and low on each side.

Life Cycle: One generation. Mature caterpillars in June. Pupa winters.

Range: Widely in eastern U.S. and southern Canada to Pacific Northwest British Columbia.

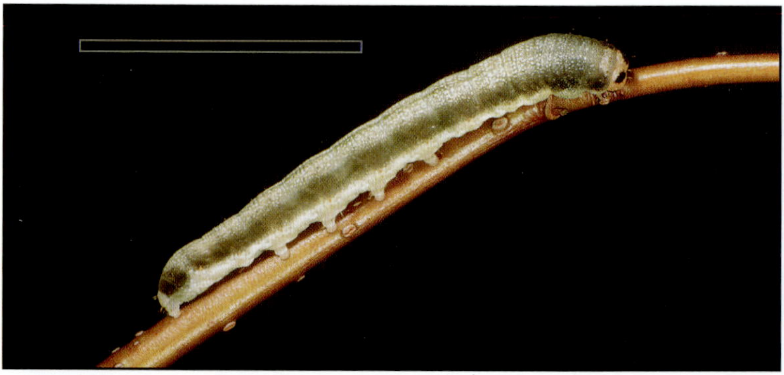

Arched Hooktip *Drepana arcuata*

APRIL	MAY	JUNE	JULY	AUG	SEPT	OCT

Caterpillar Food: Alders and birches

Moth: Forewing pale yellow-brown, with sharply-pointed, curved tips and many brown lines, including a strongly curved subterminal line.

Caterpillar: Green, mottled with brown, especially dorsally; somewhat flattened, with enlarged warts, long sparse hairs and two strong reddish bars across face. Hind prolegs fused into a short dorsal "tail."

Life Cycle: Two generations. Pupa winters.

Range: Much of Eastern U.S. and Pacific Northwest; Newfoundland to central Alaska.

Nature Notes:

Caterpillars defend leaf shelters, signaling to one another by scraping or drumming on leaf surfaces. Some pyralid caterpillars behave similarly.

Though adults resemble dead leaves, they may be chemically defended, as only two of ten moths were eaten by birds in a study.

Adults have a developed proboscis and presumably feed.

Two-lined Hooktip *Falcaria bilineata*

APRIL	MAY	JUNE	JULY	AUG	SEPT	OCT

Caterpillar Food: Paper Birch and alder; also aspen and elm

Nature Notes:

Adults are excellent dead-leaf lookalikes that sometimes hang limply by the forelegs from vegetation.

Adults have a developed proboscis and presumably feed.

Formerly *Drepana bilineata.*

Moth: Forewing pale yellow-brown, with scalloped outer margins.

Caterpillar: Orange-brown, heavily warted, head freckled, lacking bold bars across the face; hind prolegs fused into a small dorsal peg.

Life Cycle: Two generations. Pupa winters.

Range: A more northerly species with records from New England to Washington; north to central Alaska, Northwest Territories, northern Quebec, Newfoundland and Labrador. In our region, found mostly in northern forests of all three states.

Rose Hooktip *Oreta rosea*

APRIL	MAY	JUNE	JULY	AUG	SEPT	OCT

Caterpillar Food: Viburnums (especially Nannyberry) and birches

Moth: Variable. Forewings range from dull pinkish brown (inset photo) to mostly yellow with a strong subterminal yellow band. Apex hooked and postmedial line sharply angled back to costa.

Caterpillar: Brown, with knobbed head and thorax and hind prolegs fused into a long, single, tail-like extension.

Life Cycle: Two generations in much of our area, but only one further north. Pupa winters.

Range: Most of eastern U.S. to northern Minnesota; Newfoundland to Northwest Territories in Canada.

Nature Notes:

Caterpillars can be found atop viburnum leaves, where they resemble bits of dead leaf.

Adults lack a proboscis and cannot feed.

This is the only species in North America, but it is a sizable genus in Asia.

In east central Minnesota I have found grown caterpillars on June 1, strongly suggesting that eggs or caterpillars sometimes winter.

Tent Caterpillars & Lappet Moths
Family Lasiocampidae

Tent caterpillar moths (*Malacosoma* spp.) are known for their periodic population outbreaks which can have considerable ecological and economic impacts.

Moths

They are medium-sized, stout, hairy moths, cryptic in appearance. Adults cannot feed and lack tympanal hearing organs. They avoid bats through other means such as seasonal or diel temporal avoidance or flying lower to the ground. Females trend larger than males and in some species (not ours) have reduced wings. There is no frenulum/retinaculum and wing coupling is by an overlapping hindwing inner costal area expansion.

Some East Asian Lasiocampids exhibit dramatic sexual dimorphism. The small males of *Trabala pallida* are apple green but the much larger females are cadmium yellow with red medial spots.

Caterpillars

The caterpillars are hairy and many have lappets—low-set, fleshy, lateral body lobes—with hair tufts, which obscure the shadow and body outline of caterpillars. The pupae are often hairy (as in Lymantriidae).

Diversity (Species Richness/Range)

This family has over 2200 known species and is especially diverse in the Old-World tropics. There are 35 species in North America, seven or eight in our area.

Our fauna is included in two subfamilies, Lasiocampinae with 19 species in North America and Macromphaliinae with 16 species.

American Lappet Moth *Phyllodesma americana*

APRIL	MAY	JUNE	JULY	AUG	SEPT	OCT

Caterpillar Food: Especially aspen and willow

Moth: A medium-sized, gray to red-brown moth with strongly scalloped outer wing margins. Females larger than males.

Caterpillar: Gray, with abundant soft hair, especially subventrally and vague orange striping. Two red-orange transverse bands on second and third thoracic segments usually hidden.

Life Cycle: Two generations in our area. Pupa winters.

Range: Much of North America; south to Florida, Texas, Baja California; Newfoundland to Yukon, central Alaska.

Nature Notes:

Highly variable within and between populations. Summer forms tending to be redder than spring forms.

Adults have a distinctive perching posture that much resembles a crumpled dead leaf.

Caterpillars are well-camouflaged. They display their red-orange thoracic bands only when disturbed or moving.

Forest Tent Caterpillar *Malacosoma disstria*

APRIL	MAY	JUNE	JULY	AUG	SEPT	OCT

Caterpillar Food: Especially aspens & maples (except Red Maple!)

Nature Notes:

Can cause widespread defoliation of aspens. Outbreaks occur about every ten years, when the biomass of caterpillars can be astounding, by one estimate equal to that of 1800 caribou per square mile! Usually parasitoids, starvation or a virus eventually cause the population to collapse.

Western Tent Caterpillars (*Malacosoma californica*) can also be found in the boreal forest of our region.

Moth: Chunky, dull yellow to red-brown, with darker brown antemedial and postmedial lines. Median area sometimes solid brown. Females typically larger than males.

Caterpillar: Hairy, pale blue, with series of fine, irregular, orange stripes and bold series of dorsal white "key-hole" shaped marks.

Life Cycle: One generation. Winters as first-instar (pharate) caterpillar inside the egg.

Range: Most of U.S. and southern Canada; Nova Scotia to northern Alberta, British Columbia.

Eastern Tent Caterpillar *Malacosoma americanum*

APRIL	MAY	JUNE	JULY	AUG	SEPT	OCT

Caterpillar Food: Especially Black Cherry and members of rose family

Moth: Chunky, warm brown, with yellowish white antemedial and postmedial lines. Females larger than males.

Caterpillar: Hairy, complexly patterned in blue, black and white on sides, dorsum primarily orange with continuous white dorsal stripe.

Life Cycle: One generation. Winters as a first-instar pharate caterpillar within the egg. They spin a communal silk web in a fork of the food tree (inset photo above). The web acts like a greenhouse and also as a shade.

Range: Eastern two-thirds of U.S.; barely into Canada; Nova Scotia to southern Manitoba.

Nature Notes:

First-stage caterpillars contain antifreeze chemicals and do not emerge until early spring. My earliest record is April 20th in east central Minnesota.

Caterpillars are chemically defended and shunned by many birds—except the Black-billed and Yellow-billed Cuckoos, whose local population density actually increases in times of tent caterpillar outbreaks.

Large Tolype *Tolype velleda*

APRIL	MAY	JUNE	JULY	AUG	SEPT	OCT

Caterpillar Food: Many broadleaved woody plants

Nature Notes:

My records for east central Minnesota are mostly from the second week of September.

Females are larger and paler than the males.

Moth: Chunky, hairy, gray, with white veins and lines and a conspicuous thoracic tuft of curly, dark, metallic scales. Females larger, paler.

Caterpillar: Hairy, gray, flattened, with strong lappets and two rows of subdorsal warts.

Life Cycle: One generation. Eggs winter on twigs or tree trunks in linear clusters covered with dark setae from female's abdomen. Mature caterpillars spin long-tapered silk cocoons on twigs or in bark crevices.

Range: Most of eastern U.S.; across our region to southern Manitoba and Alberta.

Larch Tolype *Tolype laricis*

APRIL	MAY	JUNE	JULY	AUG	SEPT	OCT

Caterpillar Food: Conifers, especially Tamarack, Balsam Fir, spruces

Moth: Female looks like a smaller, brown version of female Large Tolype (*T. velleda*). Male is blackish gray but lacks the white wing vein markings. Unlike *T. velleda,* subterminal line shows major indented notch at halfway point.

Caterpillar: Black and gray; flattened and hairy.

Life Cycle: One generation.

Range: Northeastern U.S. and southern Canada; Nova Scotia, New England, New York, Pennsylvania north and west through our region to southern Manitoba.

Nature Notes:

This Tolype reaches further north than the Large Tolype (*T. velleda*), breeding to northern Ontario.

Males are small and dark. Fly late August through September.

Semitranslucent wings can show stunning iridescence in strong light (photo below).

Giant Silkworm Moths
Family Saturniidae

This family contains many of our largest moths. Adults rarely feed (none of ours do) and are short-lived. Adults lack hearing organs. Perhaps large size is, in part, a way to avoid small bat and bird predation. *Copiopteryx semiramus*, a tropical species, has extremely long streamers on its hindwings, perhaps to present a "too-large-to-attack" profile to foraging bats. In southern Ontario saturniids fly mostly mid May through mid June, well ahead of the July/August local peak in bat activity. They also fly less in a given night and lower to the ground. The frenulum and retinaculum are absent and wing coupling is by way of an overlapping expanded area of the basal hindwing costal area.

Moths

Adults are often quite large and tend toward sexual dimorphism, with smaller males specialized to find females and larger females specialized for delivering large egg loads to food plants. Since they are short-lived and do not feed, males and females (unlike most adult hawk moths) do not have common needs (such as feeding at flowers) that moderate dimorphism.

Caterpillars

Many caterpillars are protected by urticating hairs and spines. Compared with hawk moths, saturniids lay larger eggs and their caterpillars have broader diets, often on mature foliage. They have simple jaws that snip out discs of leaf that are not well "chewed." Their head capsules are relatively small. They grow more slowly and rely less on visually matching their food plants and more on defenses such as stinging spines or mimicry of stinging spines.

Some of our species have long larval food plant lists, but often with distinct preferences (e.g. Cecropia Moths prefer maples). Others are regional specialists (our Luna Moths eat Paper Birch, but in the southern U.S., mostly walnuts). Others are more specialized (Columbia Silk Moths feed only on Tamarack through most of their range).

Many species pupate in strong silken cocoons on plants or in leaf-litter.

Diversity (Species Richness/Range)

Worldwide there are over 1300 species with highest diversity in tropical America. Presently there are eight recognized world subfamilies, three represented by 78 species, including about 17 in our area, present in North America. Our species are contained in three subfamilies: Ceratocampinae with 22 species, Hemileucinae with 36 and Saturniinae with 20.

Canadian Imperial Moth *Eacles pini*

APRIL	MAY	JUNE	JULY	AUG	SEPT	OCT

Caterpillar Food: Conifers; especially Red Pine and White Pine

Moth: Large yellow moths with much purplish, pinkish, or orangish shading, especially in the basal areas. Shading stronger in males.

Caterpillar: Large and plump with long silky hairs, showy white spiracles, and paired spine-like horns on second and third thoracic segments.

Life Cycle: One generation. Pupa winters.

Range: In pine forests through much of the northern Great Lakes, including the northern third of lower Michigan and Ontario north of Lakes Huron and Superior to the Minnesota border at the west end of its range.

Nature Notes:

Females call after midnight, especially 1 to 2:30 a.m.

Recently split off from the Pine Imperial Moth, *Eacles imperialis*, as a distinct species. Pine Imperial Moth is larger and more heavily marked. It ranges from Costa Rica to southern Wisconsin, Michigan and southeast Minnesota.

Pink-striped Oakworm *Anisota virginiensis*

APRIL	MAY	JUNE	JULY	AUG	SEPT	OCT

Caterpillar Food: Oaks

Nature Notes:

Mating occurs late morning. If daytime mating has been favored to avoid bat predation (they can't hear bats) it must come at a price in terms of bird predation. Extremely rapid flight and the bee-like appearance of males may counter this.

Yellow-orange eggs are laid on the underside of oak leaves in clusters of up to one hundred. Young caterpillars feed communally.

Moth: Sexes differ greatly: males have narrow, brown, angular wings, with large transparent areas in the forewing. The larger females have broader, orange-brown wings with a heavy pink tinge beyond postmedial line.

Caterpillar: Pink and black striped caterpillar, with many white dots and short black spines and black tentacles on the thorax.

Life Cycle: One generation in our area. Pupa winters underground.

Range: Most of eastern U.S.; northwest range limit Minnesota, southeast Manitoba.

Rosy Maple Moth *Dryocampa rubicunda*

APRIL	MAY	JUNE	JULY	AUG	SEPT	OCT

Caterpillar Food: Red Maple, Sugar Maple and Silver Maple

Moth: Usually yellow body and wings with bright pink covering all but median area of forewing, but sometimes absent. Females have simple and males bipectinate, antennae.

Caterpillar: Green with many broad pale stripes and black tentacles from second thoracic segment. Rosy patch low on seventh and eighth abdominal segments.

Life Cycle: One generation in our area. Pupa winters in a shallow underground cell.

Range: Eastern U.S. onto edge of Great Plains and southern edge of Canada; Nova Scotia to Minnesota and adjacent Ontario.

Nature Notes:

Caterpillars are sometimes numerous enough to defoliate maples.

Adults emerge in late afternoon or evening. Mating occurs about 10 p.m. to midnight, pairs remaining together through the next day. Yellow eggs are laid in clusters of ten to 30 and hatch in about two weeks. Young caterpillars feed together, but become solitary.

Buck Moths *Hemileuca maia* group

APRIL	MAY	JUNE	JULY	AUG	SEPT	OCT

Caterpillar Food: *H. nevadensis*—Willows, aspen, Bog Birch

Nature Notes:

Taxonomy of the *Hemileucas* is complex and ongoing. Identification in the field often based on range, food plants, caterpillar traits.

Eastern Buck Moth, *H. maia,* eat mostly oaks; Bogbean Buck Moth, *H. menyanthevora,* specializes on its namesake plant.

Populations local but can be abundant. Adults fly on sunny days in early autumn.

Caterpillars may feed on the invasive Purple Loosestrife.

Moth: Attractive black moths with white bands in the median area. Females have more red-orange on tip of abdomen.

Caterpillar: CAUTION: venomous to the touch, spines delivering a painful sting.

Life Cycle: One generation. Egg winters. But up to fifty percent of pupae may undergo prolonged diapause through a second winter.

Range: *H. nevadensis* from southwest U.S. to Minnesota. *H. menyanthevora* only in southern Wisconsin in our area. *H. maia* from eastern Minnesota to New England, Florida.

Io Moth *Automeris io*

APRIL	MAY	JUNE	JULY	AUG	SEPT	OCT

Caterpillar Food: Strongly associated with oaks in our region

Moth: Males in our area have mostly bright yellow forewings, female forewings are reddish brown. Hindwings largely yellow, each with a large, dark spot resembling a vertebrate eye, complete with highlights.

Caterpillar: Green, with red and white spiracular stripes and many clusters of branched, pale green, stinging spines.

Life Cycle: One generation in our area. Pupa winters in a papery cocoon in leaf litter.

Range: Eastern U.S. to mountains of Colorado; New England to southern Manitoba in the north and south to Costa Rica.

Nature Notes:

One of our most common saturniids. Adults fly mostly from 10 pm to midnight.

Beware of touching the caterpillar, whose sting resembles that of nettles.

When disturbed, the bold patterns and bright colors of the wings are flashed into view. Recent study suggests that a bold pattern, rather than a resemblance to eyes, startles predators.

Polyphemus Moth *Antheraea polyphemus*

APRIL	MAY	JUNE	JULY	AUG	SEPT	OCT

Caterpillar Food: Favors birch, willow, maple and oak

Nature Notes:

Caterpillars can make snapping or rasping sounds by rubbing their mandibles together when disturbed. The clicking includes frequencies audible to birds and bats. Some bats might be repelled by the ultrasonic frequencies; as might some rodent predators, such as Deer Mice which also hear ultrasound.

"Polyphemus" refers to the one-eyed giant son of Poseidon in Greek mythology.

Moth: Large, with red-to-yellow brown wings. An oval transparent spot on each wing ringed with yellow, black and blue. Wingspan to 6 inches.

Caterpillar: Plump, green with silvery-red warts, pale yellowish lines slanting through spiracles. Lacks the pale yellow subspiracular line of the luna caterpillar.

Life Cycle: One generation in our area. Pupa winters in a flimsy cocoon on the food plant or in leaf litter.

Range: Most of U.S. and central Canada; our area all the way to the Northwest Territories.

Luna Moth *Actias luna*

APRIL	MAY	JUNE	JULY	AUG	SEPT	OCT

Caterpillar Food: In our area strongly favoring Paper Birch

Moth: Large, pale-green, with long, sweeping, hindwing tails and a transparent spot ringed with pink on each wing.

Caterpillar: Large, plump, beautiful green, with bright red warts and spiracles. Transverse yellow lines run vertically along intersegmental creases between first to eighth segments.

Life Cycle: One generation in our area. Pupa winters in a papery brown cocoon spun in leaf litter near the base of the food plant.

Range: Most of eastern U.S. and southern Canada; our area to northern Alberta.

Nature Notes:

Spurs at the base of the wings assist in exiting the cocoon, which lacks a well-defined escape valve.

The pupa has a clear "window" through which even dim light can stimulate the brain. Photoperiod likely contributes to breaking diapause. If a cocoon is moved, the pupa within may noisily reorient itself to the light.

Actias is a mostly Asian genus, with about 23 species.

Promethea Moth *Callosamia promethea*

APRIL	MAY	JUNE	JULY	AUG	SEPT	OCT

Caterpillar Food: Especially Black Cherry and ashes; perhaps lilac

Nature Notes:

Males can fly over 20 miles during their week-long lives.

The dark, day-flying, males may mimic unpalatable swallowtail butterflies to deter attack by birds.

Seems to have declined in numbers, perhaps due to the tachinid fly parasitoid (*Compsilura concinnata*) introduced in a (failed) attempt to control Spongy Moths (*Lymantria dispar*).

Moth: Sexually dimorphic. Wings are blackish with tan outer borders in males. Females are reddish brown, much paler outside the conspicuous white postmedial line.

Caterpillar: Pale green, with four red knobs on thorax and one yellow knob on eighth abdominal segment. Several rows of dark blue warts circled with pale blue.

Life Cycle: One generation in our area. Pupa winters on the food plant in a slender, long-"stemmed," silk cocoon (inset below).

Range: Most of eastern U.S.; reaches its northwest U.S. range limit in northern Minnesota.

Tulip-tree Silkmoth *Callosamia angulifera*

APRIL	MAY	JUNE	JULY	AUG	SEPT	OCT

Caterpillar Food: Tulip-tree (Yellow Poplar) of the Magnolia family

Moth: Sexually dimorphic. Male upperside brown and contrasty; angular white marks on all wings. Male's underside has a broad pale band to the outside of the postmedian line. Female upperside yellowish brown; her white spots are largest on the forewings.

Caterpillar: Similar to Promethea but lacks obvious black spots. Dark brown cocoon in curled leaf that falls to ground.

Life Cycle: One generation in our area.

Range: Over much of eastern U.S.; only southernmost Michigan in our region.

Nature Notes:

Peak mating activity around 10pm.

Female similar to female Promethea Moth (opposite page) but Tulip-tree Silkmoth's angular white spots are larger on forewings than hindwings; opposite on Promethea.

Cecropia Moth *Hyalophora cecropia*

APRIL	MAY	JUNE	JULY	AUG	SEPT	OCT

Caterpillar Food: Many woody plants; favors maples

Nature Notes:

Largest moth in the U.S. and Canada by wing surface area with broad wings spreading up to 6 inches. Female Black Witch (*Ascalapha odorata*; pg 190) has narrower wings but hers can span 8 inches!

Males may fly more than 20 miles over several nights, mating with several females. Populations sometimes sparse, likely only a few adults per square mile.

Some suburban populations may be quite dense.

Moth: Large, with red body and white collar. Wings dark brown with red shadings in basal area, eyespots and outside the strong white postmedial line. Wingspan 4 to 6 inches.

Caterpillar: Plump, pale bluish-green, with rows of yellow, orange and blue knobs. Early instars dark (inset photo below).

Life Cycle: One generation. Pupa winters in a tough silk cocoon on vegetation (not always the food plant)(inset photo below).

Range: Most of eastern U.S.; Newfoundland to southern Manitoba.

Columbia Silkmoth *Hyalophora columbia*

APRIL	MAY	JUNE	JULY	AUG	SEPT	OCT

Caterpillar Food: exclusively Tamarack in our region

Moth: Purple to brick red upperwings. Smaller than Cecropia and lacks red shading in the reniform spot, discal spot and postmedial line.

Caterpillar: Similar to Cecropia. Plump, green with prominent rows of tubercles.

Life Cycle: One generation. Overwinters as pupa.

Range: Across northern New England and southern Quebec to northwest Ontario and Manitoba; south to the northern Tamarack bog forests in our region.

Nature Notes:

A boreal bog species. Eastern range defined by the presence of its only caterpillar host, Tamarack.

Lumped with Glover's Silkmoth (ssp. *gloveri*) of the Rocky Mountain states and western plains, but many consider them separate species due to almost no range overlap and habitat differences. Website iNaturalist treats them as separate species.

Sphinx Moths (Hawk Moths) Family Sphingidae

This family is usually placed in the superfamily Bombycoidea. In most species the adults feed on nectar while hovering and have extremely acute color vision, even in deepest darkness. They have relatively large brains, allowing them to track productive nectar sources. "Pit organs" on the labial palps are sensitive to carbon dioxide and help guide nectar feeders to the most productive sources. Hawk moths are important pollinators of trees in the tropics and of orchids throughout the world. They also drink water from pools and streams. Nectar sugars and water extend the lifespan, supply flight fuel and some (but not all) of the amino acids needed for egg production. Most members of the Smerinthinae have reduced mouth parts and do not feed and these have shorter lives and lay their eggs sooner after mating, in fewer, larger batches. Apparently in North America only the White-lined Sphinx (*Hyles lineata*) is equipped with hearing (on its mouthparts!). Large size, rapid flight and restricted hours of flight in part compensate to avoid predation by bats in the many species that lack hearing. A few in our area avoid bats by flying early in the year or during the day. Some tropical species have very sharp, sturdy spurs on their hindlegs, able to stab a predator's mouth (or a lepidopterist's hand!).

Moths

Medium-sized to very large, long-lived strong-flying moths with narrow forewings. While many species come readily to lights, others rarely or never do, even some that are nocturnal. Most species are crepuscular or nocturnal, but a few fly only in full daylight.

Caterpillars

Compared with giant silk moth caterpillars, sphingids have more toxic, specialized diets, "chew" their food more carefully, grow more rapidly and visually blend in better with their food plants. Their eggs are much smaller than those of silk moths and the caterpillar head capsules are relatively more massive to support the larger jaws and chewing muscles.

Diversity (Species Richness/Range)

There are about 1100 species worldwide and they are especially diverse in the tropics. North America has 131 species and our area about 45 (including several very rare strays). The family has long been divided into the subfamilies Sphinginae with 63 North American species and Macroglossinae with 66. Another subfamily, Smerinthinae, is sometimes split from the Sphinginae.

Pawpaw Sphinx *Dolba hyloeus*

APRIL	MAY	JUNE	JULY	AUG	SEPT	OCT

Caterpillar Food: Winterberry in our area

Moth: Forewing dark brown, with black lines and a dusting of white. Hindwing black, with white median line.

Caterpillar: Pale bluish green, with seven slanting white lines edged with pink and blue, hindmost running onto bluish horn.

Life Cycle: One generation in our area. Mature caterpillars July to September. Pupa winters.

Range: Much of eastern U.S. into southernmost Canada; southern edge of our area; U.P. of Michigan. Few records for Minnesota. I have seen only two in east central Minnesota.

Nature Notes:

My two records from east central Minnesota came to a mercury-vapor light on July 16 and 17, 2005.

Adults come to lights (though perhaps not often) and visit flowers for nectar at dusk.

Tuttle (2007) shorts the northwestern extent of the range, though to what extent remains unknown.

Waved Sphinx *Ceratomia undulosa*

APRIL	MAY	JUNE	JULY	AUG	SEPT	OCT

Caterpillar Food: Ash species in our area

Nature Notes:

This is a food plant specialist that could be harmed by the looming approach of the introduced Emerald Ash Borer beetle, which has killed around 30 million ash trees of all species and age-classes in Michigan.

In eastern Ontario a distinctly bimodal flight was reported, with peaks in mid June and mid July.

Moth: Forewing pale gray-brown, with many black streaks and zigzags and large white reniform dots ringed in black.

Caterpillar: Pale yellow-green dorsally and blue-green laterally, with seven slanting white lines, a long pinkish caudal horn, head with two strong white vertical bands. Strong black spots on anal plate. Spiracles red.

Life Cycle: One generation in our area. Pupa winters in a cell several inches underground.

Range: Eastern two-thirds of North America; Nova Scotia to Alberta, south to Mexico.

Hermit Sphinx *Lintneria eremitus*

APRIL	MAY	JUNE	JULY	AUG	SEPT	OCT

Caterpillar Food: Herbs in the mint family, such as bergamot

Moth: Forewing gray-brown, with black dashes and zigzag lines. Reniform spot white, sometimes double. Hindwing black, with two broad white bands and a black basal triangle.

Caterpillar: Mottled brown and green, with a large black oval over second and third thoracic segments. Second segment strongly humped.

Life Cycle: One generation in our area. Pupa winters in a cell in the soil.

Range: Northeastern species; New England south in mountains to Georgia. Reaches northwest range limit in Minnesota, possibly southeast Manitoba.

Nature Notes:

Best found at dusk, feeding at various flowers, or as a caterpillar (at night) on mint species.

A patch of flowering milkweeds or dogbanes is a good place to watch for hawk moths at dusk.

Caterpillars hide during the day near the base of food plants and climb at dusk to feed at night; thus they are easily overlooked.

Laurel Sphinx *Sphinx kalmiae*

APRIL	MAY	JUNE	JULY	AUG	SEPT	OCT

Caterpillar Food: In our area, mostly ash; also birches and lilac

Nature Notes:

Adults feed at flowers.

My four caterpillar records from east central Minnesota range from September 22 through 28. All were found on ash saplings along forest edges. Whether this reflects an egg placement preference by females or a mere sampling bias (easier to find there than up in grown ash trees) is unknown.

Also known as Fawn Sphinx.

Moth: Forewing mostly pale yellowish brown, with dark brown to black along inner margin and along inside of conspicuous white subterminal line.

Caterpillar: Green, with seven slanting yellow lines bordered above with black. Caudal horn blue, covered with small black spines.

Life Cycle: One generation in our area. Pupa winters underground.

Range: Most of eastern U.S. and southern edge of Canada; Newfoundland to Saskatchewan.

Apple Sphinxes *Sphinx poecila/gordius*

APRIL	MAY	JUNE	JULY	AUG	SEPT	OCT

Caterpillar Food: Tamarack, Sweet Gale, meadowsweet & blueberries

Moth: Both species are medium-sized, gray, with black streaking, a wavy black postmedial line and a white reniform spot. Hindwing black, crossed by wavy whitish band.

Caterpillar: Usually green (sometimes reddish), with seven slanting white lines edged with blackish red. Numerous tiny black rings below the spiracles and over the thorax.

Life Cycle: One generation. Pupa winters underground.

Range: Northern Apple Sphinx widely through Canada, south into northern U.S.

Nature Notes:

Northern Apple Sphinx (*S. poecila*) has long been confused with Apple Sphinx (*S. gordius*), which is more southerly, (reaches the southern fringe of our area) but does overlap with *poecila* in the Great Lakes area. It is now known that the two cannot be identified with any assurance in the field; DNA is the only reliable method.

Northern Apple Sphinx is likely the most common hawk moth in Canada.

Clemen's Sphinx *Sphinx luscitiosa*

APRIL	MAY	JUNE	JULY	AUG	SEPT	OCT

Caterpillar Food: Willows, birches; also Bog Rosemary & blueberries

Nature Notes:

One of several sphinx moths most closely associated with boreal forest.

Adults feed at flowers and carrion at dusk or mid day. Females regularly appear at lights, males much less often. Mating activity has been observed in daylight and at dusk.

Distribution appears to be patchy (local).

Moth: Male's forewing yellow-brown, female's gray; black shading beyond the postmedial line broadens toward inner margin. Hindwing deep yellow in male and pale yellow in female; outer border broadly banded in black in both.

Caterpillar: Pale green, with seven bold white slanting lines, each bordered above with deep purple. Caudal horn black dorsally, green below.

Life Cycle: One generation. Pupa winters several inches underground.

Range: Across northeastern U.S. and southern Canada with broad lobe to central Alaska and a southern lobe through Rocky Mountains.

Northern Pine Sphinx *Lapara bombycoides*

APRIL	MAY	JUNE	JULY	AUG	SEPT	OCT

Caterpillar Food: Pines (Jack, White & Red) but also Tamarack

Moth: Forewing dull gray, marked by black dashes and zigzag lines. Females larger and less strongly marked than males.

Caterpillar: Green, with white subdorsal, lateral and subspiracular stripes and reddish dorsal markings. The head is triangular, red with yellow lines. Spiracles are black with pale rims.

Life Cycle: One generation in our area. Pupa winters in a shallow underground chamber.

Range: Broadly along northern tier of states and south edge of Canada from Atlantic to Minnesota and extending northwest to Alberta and south in the Appalachians.

Nature Notes:

The striped green caterpillars blend in well among pine needles.

Males come to lights much more often than females.

There are three *Lapara* species in North America, all confined to the East. This is the only one in our region.

Twin-spotted Sphinx *Smerinthus jamaicensis*

APRIL	MAY	JUNE	JULY	AUG	SEPT	OCT

Caterpillar Food: Especially willows, also poplars and elms

Nature Notes:

Adults do not feed, come readily to light and are reported to fly after midnight (in Arkansas; whether this pertains here is unknown).

Caterpillars sometimes regurgitate crop contents when disturbed.

There are ten species in this holarctic genus; three occur in North America, two in our area.

Moth: Distinctive is a dark hemisphere, banded with white, at the tip of the forewing. Hindwing washed with red, with a blue eyespot bordered in black and often bisected by a black bar (can also be undivided or doubly-divided).

Caterpillar: Bluish to yellowish green, with a rough bluish caudal horn and six slanting white lateral stripes. Many raised white granules.

Life Cycle: One generation in our area. Pupa winters shallow in soil.

Range: Most of eastern U.S., Great Plains. In Canada from Newfoundland to Yukon.

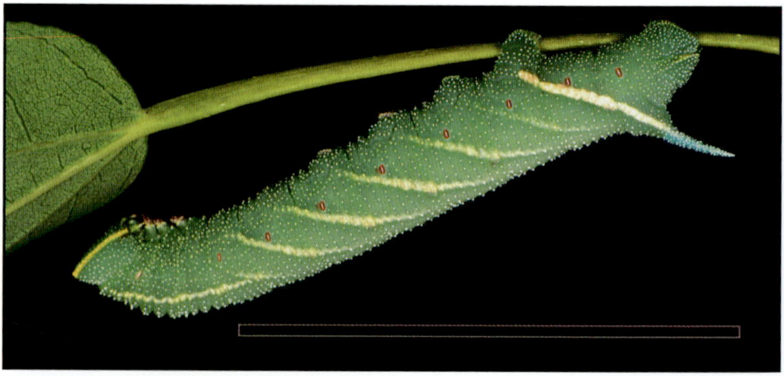

One-eyed Sphinx *Smerinthus cerisyi*

APRIL	MAY	JUNE	JULY	AUG	SEPT	OCT

Caterpillar Food: Willows and poplars

Moth: Hindwing reddish with a blue eyespot ringed and bull's-eyed with black. Highly variable in size and scalloping in populations.

Caterpillar: Resembles that of Twin-spotted Sphinx but has a well-developed white subdorsal line that continues nearly to the last lateral stripe. Caudal horn is often pink.

Life Cycle: One generation in our area. Pupa winters shallow in soil.

Range: Northern states and southern Canada in east, expanding greatly north and south to Alaska and Mexico in West.

Nature Notes:

This is one of the hawk moths most closely associated with boreal forest.

The early flight season avoids peak bat activity in mid to late summer.

Adults do not feed, but come well to lights.

Note perching posture (inset) that is common to many sphinx moths.

Blinded Sphinx *Paonias excaecata*

APRIL	MAY	JUNE	JULY	AUG	SEPT	OCT

Caterpillar Food: Many broadleaved woody plants (regional preferences)

Nature Notes:

May be called "Blinded" because hindwing eyespots have no central black spots or "pupil."

Adults are apparently unable to feed.

Dead adults were readily eaten by birds in one study.

Also known as Blind-eyed Sphinx.

Moth: Forewing shades of brown, with strongly scalloped outer edge. Hindwing reddish, with blue eyespot ringed with black.

Caterpillar: Green, with many white granular spots, seven white diagonal lateral stripes, caudal horn green, spiracles white, rimmed with black.

Life Cycle: One generation in our area. Pupa winters shallow in soil.

Range: Most of eastern U.S. and Great Plains, parts of West to Pacific and southern Canada; Nova Scotia to northern Alberta and British Columbia.

Small-eyed Sphinx *Paonias myops*

APRIL	MAY	JUNE	JULY	AUG	SEPT	OCT

Caterpillar Food: Especially cherry; also hawthorns & juneberries

Moth: Forewing dark to light brown, with outer margins broadly and doubly indented. Hindwing more or less deep yellow with a black-bordered, pale blue, eye-spot.

Caterpillar: Bright green, often with subdorsal red spots on second and seventh abdominal segments. The caudal horn is short, straight and green.

Life Cycle: One generation in our area. Pupa winters underground.

Range: Most of U.S. and across southern Canada; Nova Scotia to British Columbia.

Nature Notes:

Most northern records from mid June to mid July.

Perched with the abdomen arched, this moth resembles a curled dry leaf.

A holarctic genus of four species, three in North America.

Big Poplar Sphinx *Pachysphinx modesta*

APRIL	MAY	JUNE	JULY	AUG	SEPT	OCT

Caterpillar Food: Poplars (especially) and willows

Nature Notes:

Caterpillars chew through leaf petioles to remove partly-eaten leaves, reducing visual evidence of their presence.

Adults somewhat resemble dried poplar leaves. When disturbed they display maroon-red hindwing patches. Size alone likely confers some protection against smaller birds and bats.

Also known as Modest Sphinx.

Moth: Unmistakably large; forewings shades of gray, with strongly scalloped outer margin; hindwings with much red.

Caterpillar: Stout, pale blue-green, with a series of white lines slanting upward and back, red spiracular markings and a small caudal horn.

Life Cycle: One generation in our area. Pupa winters several inches below ground.

Range: Most of eastern three-quarters of U.S. and southern half of Canada reaching as far north as southern Northwest Territories. South to Texas and Florida.

Walnut Sphinx *Amorpha juglandis*

APRIL	MAY	JUNE	JULY	AUG	SEPT	OCT

Caterpillar Food: In our area hop hornbeam (Ironwood) and hazel

Moth: Forewing shades of pale to dark brown, with white-edged antemedial and postmedial lines. All wings with wavy margins.

Caterpillar: Green, conspicuously dotted with white granules ringed with black. Spiracles orange with a white spot at top and bottom. Head pointed and strongly edged in white.

Life Cycle: One generation. Caterpillars mature mid summer to early fall. Pupa winters.

Range: Eastern U.S. and southern edge of Canada; northwest range limit is Manitoba.

Nature Notes:

The caterpillar is conspicuous in its ability to make loud squeaking sounds, apparently by forcing air through its spiracles, while violently thrashing side to side and even biting!

Adults perch with their abdomens arched and wings partly spread, resembling dead brown leaves (inset photo).

Titan Sphinx *Aellopos titan*

APRIL	MAY	JUNE	JULY	AUG	SEPT	OCT

Caterpillar Food: Buttonbush & others in the madder family (Rubiaceae)

Nature Notes:

Mainly a vagrant into our region and most often recorded from mid August to October.

Much longer flight period than Nessus Sphinx (*Amphion floridensis*) (facing page).

Genus name *Aellopos* from the Greek for "storm-footed" or "swift."

Moth: Overall brown with single white band across wide abdomen that is easily seen in flight. Pale bands across forewings.

Caterpillar: Green (or brown) with seven slanting lines; posterior line black-edged pinkish-red. Long bluish caudal horn.

Life Cycle: One generation. Caterpillars burrow into the soil to pupate.

Range: Widely across the eastern U.S. and south through Central and South America to Argentina; all of our region to southeast Manitoba.

Nessus Sphinx *Amphion floridensis*

APRIL	MAY	JUNE	JULY	AUG	SEPT	OCT

Caterpillar Food: Grape (*Vitis* species)

Moth: Pair of yellow bands on stout abdomen are easily noted in the field. Brown above; rusty orange underwings. Also reddish-organge markings on side of abdomen.

Caterpillar: Final instar mottled brown with diagonal darker brown lines on each segment; horn short and black. Earlier instars green.

Life Cycle: One generation. Caterpillars pupate in underground chambers.

Range: Widely across the eastern U.S. southern Canada to central Quebec; all of our region to southeast Manitoba.

Nature Notes:

Much more commonly recorded on iNaturalist than Titan Sphinx (*Aellopos titan;* opposite page).

Flight period mostly limited to late May to mid June in our region.

Hummingbird Clearwing *Hemaris thysbe*

APRIL	MAY	JUNE	JULY	AUG	SEPT	OCT

Caterpillar Food: Especially viburnums; also blueberries, cranberries

Nature Notes:

The similar Slender Clearwing (*H. gracilis*) is smaller, has all red legs, and lacks "veins" across a small forewing cell. Late May through June.

Commonly seen in full daylight, hovering at flowers of milkweeds, thistles, petunias, dogbanes, phlox, mints, etc.

Though sometimes mistaken for a hummingbird by humans, they may mimic bumblebees.

Moth: Body yellowish brown, wings brown, with large, transparent, unscaled areas.

Caterpillar: Lime green (less often reddish). Yellow on front edge of thorax, subdorsal stripe and base of prolegs. Head and body sprinkled with tiny white spots. Horn curved and bluish.

Life Cycle: One generation in our area. Pupa winters in a flimsy cocoon in leaf litter.

Range: Most of eastern U.S. and much of southern and western Canada, into Northwest Territories and central Alaska.

Diervilla Clearwing *Hemaris aethra*

APRIL	MAY	JUNE	JULY	AUG	SEPT	OCT

Caterpillar Food: Northern Bush Honeysuckle (*Diervilla lonicera*)

Moth: This species has more distinctly red wingtips and an uninterrupted yellow abdomen tip compared to Snowberry Clearwing (brownish wingtips, black edged abdomen tip).

Caterpillar: Red spiracular spots circled with black; caudal horn with reddish base. In *H. diffinis*, black spiracular spots and caudal horn with a yellow base (photo below).

Life Cycle: Pupa winters in a cocoon of silk.

Range: Only in boreal forest from Manitoba, Minnesota to Maine, Nova Scotia. Snowberry Clearwing across eastern U.S.

Nature Notes:

Formerly included with Snowberry Clearwing (*Hemaris diffinis*), this species is now resurrected back to full species status (as it was 100 years ago!). It is found in northern parts of our region where its caterpillar feeds on Northern Bush Honeysuckle.

Adults are strictly day-active and frequently seen at various flowers. Their resemblance to bumblebees may protect against feeding birds. Nickname: "bumblebee moth."

Snowberry Clearwing caterpillar
Hemaris diffinis

Abbott's Sphinx *Sphecodina abbottii*

APRIL	MAY	JUNE	JULY	AUG	SEPT	OCT

Caterpillar Food: Grapes and woodbine (Virginia Creeper) in our area

Nature Notes:

Both caterpillar forms are highly cryptic, one on woody vines, the other among green tendrils, leaves and unripe fruits. Brown form feeds at night, resting on woody vines during the day. The green form feeds day and night, resting closer to the foliage. Tend to eat an entire leaf before moving on.

Adults feed at flowers, mud, dung, carrion and tree sap flows.

Moth: Forewings dark brown with scalloped outer edges. Hindwing with a broad yellow band. Males have a "fantail," females a pointed caudal tuft of scales.

Caterpillar: Two distinct forms; one finely striped with black, white and brown; the other with similar background broken by large green patches dorsally and laterally. Caudal horn replaced in final instar by a shiny black eye-like button.

Life Cycle: One generation. Pupa winters.

Range: Most of eastern U.S. and southern edge of Canada; New Brunswick to Manitoba.

White-lined Sphinx *Hyles lineata*

APRIL	MAY	JUNE	JULY	AUG	SEPT	OCT

Caterpillar Food: Especially evening primroses (*Oenothera*) in our area

Moth: Forewing shows whitish stripe running base to tip and crossed by about six white lines on veins. Three pairs of white lines on the thorax. Hindwing black, with broad pink band.

Caterpillar: Highly variable contrasting pattern of green or yellow and black. Head, thoracic shield and anal plate all same color (green or orange). Caudal horn yellow or orange.

Life Cycle: One generation in our area. Pupa winters in loose cocoon at or near the surface.

Range: All of U.S. and southern Canada, south to Argentina; Nova Scotia to British Columbia.

Nature Notes:

Adults feed at flowers, mainly at dusk, but also mid day.

Unable to survive winter in our area, requiring it to immigrate each year from further south. Undergoes remarkable fluctuations in abundance, but tends to be uncommon in our area.

Gallium Sphinx (*Hyles gallii*) also occurs here. It lacks white cross streaking on wings and thorax. Caterpillar feeds on Bedstraws (*Galium spp*).

Virginia Creeper Sphinx *Darapsa myron*

APRIL	MAY	JUNE	JULY	AUG	SEPT	OCT

Caterpillar Food: Grape and woodbine (Virginia Creeper) in our area

Nature Notes:

Formerly known as "Hog Sphinx" but origin of the common name has eluded me. Is it for the "jowly" appearance of the caterpillar?

Adults feed at flowers and come to sugar bait and lights.

Strangely, this species established a vastly disjunct breeding population in Thailand, which was discovered quite by accident in 1991.

Moth: Overall olive-green caste. Hindwing mostly unmarked, reddish.

Caterpillar: Blue-green or brown with a small head and enlarged thorax and a clearly defined dark subdorsal stripe that separates pale lateral striping from a darker dorsal saddle. Caudal horn is curved and often pink.

Life Cycle: Possibly a partial second generation. Pupa winters in a loose cocoon at or just below ground.

Range: Most of eastern U.S.; northwest to northern Minnesota; rare in the North Woods.

Azalea Sphinx *Darapsa choerilus*

APRIL	MAY	JUNE	JULY	AUG	SEPT	OCT

Caterpillar Food: In our area mostly viburnums; also blueberries

Moth: Forewing similar to Hog Sphinx, but with a pale reddish caste and deeper purplish bands. Hindwing reddish.

Caterpillar: Green or brown with a straight blue-green caudal horn.

Life Cycle: Likely one generation in our area. Pupa winters in a silk cocoon in leaf litter.

Range: Most of eastern U.S. and southern edge of Canada, extending to northwestern Alberta and southern Northwest Territories; our area to central Ontario, southern Manitoba.

Nature Notes:

Adults feed at flowers and sugar bait and come to lights.

There are three known *Darapsa* species, all North American.

Formerly known as *Darapsa pholus.*

Uranias & Scoopwings Family Uraniidae

Uraniids were once included in Geometridae, based largely on the shared presence of abdominal tympanal hearing organs, but are now considered distinct based on differences in the structure and positioning of these "ears" from those of geometrids.

Moths

Ours are small drably-colored moths called scoopwings for their distinctive perching postures, with the forewings rolled and/or held away from the hindwings. The tympanal hearing organs (ears) are sexually dimorphic, located on the first abdominal segment in females and on the second abdominal segment in males. The proboscis is developed and adults presumably feed. Wings are coupled by a frenulum and retinaculum.

Caterpillars

Scoopwing caterpillars are small, plump and drab, with sparse, short setae arising from low wide warts. Their prolegs are very small.

Diversity (Species Richness/Range)

Uraniidae contains two subfamilies: Uraniinae with about 100 species, mostly tropical, large and showy (they have been confused with swallowtail butterflies!) and not occurring in North America; and Epipleminae with about 600 species, also mostly tropical and represented by ten species in North America, including two in our area.

Brown Scoopwing *Calledapteryx dryopterata*

APRIL	MAY	JUNE	JULY	AUG	SEPT	OCT

Caterpillar Food: Viburnums; perhaps especially Nannyberry

Moth: Wings shades of brown with large scallops, those on the forewings lined with dark brown. The perching posture is highly distinctive.

Caterpillar: Stout gray, with many low, pale-ringed warts; head with many dark markings.

Life Cycle: Two generations over much of range; possibly one here. Pupa winters in leaf litter.

Range: Much of eastern U.S. and southern Ontario; Maine to Minnesota. South to Brazil. Few records in our three-state region.

Nature Notes:

Younger caterpillars feed together in leaf shelters.

Adults have pale and dark forms. In their distinctive resting posture they resemble tattered fragments of dead leaf.

Gray Scoopwing (*Callizzia amorata*) has same "scoop-wing shape" but is more distinctly patterned with browns and tans; brown triangle mark along trailing edge of forewing.

Inchworms & Geometer Moths Family Geometridae

While the taxonomy is less unsettled than that of Noctuoidea, the subfamily classification is suspect and much change is expected.

Moths

Adults have slender bodies and relatively large wings. Some northern species are able to fly with body temperatures near freezing. Some females have only tiny nubs for wings. Tympanal hearing organs (ears) are present (except in wingless females) on the base of the abdomen and facing forward, each supplied by four sensory neurons. The proboscis is well developed and most adults presumably feed.

Caterpillars

The caterpillars are more or less twig-like with (almost always) only two pairs of prolegs. Some species have either an undersized third pair on the fifth abdominal segment, or even a full set of five pairs.

And some overwintering Geometrid caterpillars are a rich source of winter protein for certain birds in our region. Golden-crowned Kinglets and Black-capped Chickadees seek out these tiny caterpillars. In fact, it is highly unlikely that the kinglets could even winter in the North without the food source. Biologist Bernd Heinrich discovered that Golden-crowned Kinglets in Maine gorged on One-spotted Variant (*Hypagyrtis unipunctata*) caterpillars that they gleaned from tree branches.

Diversity (Species Richness/Range)

A huge family of about 23,000 known species worldwide, in eight subfamilies, including 1415 species in five (or six) subfamilies in North America. (Alsophilinae is still on the North American checklist, but sunk into Ennominae on the World checklist.) Six subfamilies are recognized in North America: Alsophilinae (three spp.), Archiearinae (three spp.), Ennominae (74 spp.), Larentiinae (470 spp.), Sterrhinae (96 spp.), and all are represented in our region.

Chickweed Geometer *Haematopis grataria*

APRIL	MAY	JUNE	JULY	AUG	SEPT	OCT

Caterpillar Food: Chickweeds, clovers, smartweeds & many others

Moth: A cheery day flier with bright yellow wings marked with pinkish lines and spots. Males have feathery antennae.

Caterpillar: Slender, somewhat enlarged at the first abdominal segment; coloration highly variable, often green and white striped or mottled with reddish brown.

Life Cycle: Several to many generations in much of range; unknown in our area. Pupa winters.

Range: Much of eastern North America west to Alberta; southern part of our region.

Nature Notes:

The palatability of this bright moth to birds seems unknown.

My latest Minnesota records to mid September.

The Sweetfern Geometer (below) is a melanistic (dark form) specimen. Often adults are paler to white. Caterpillar feeds on Sweetfern and Tamarack. It has a chrysalis-type pupae. Found mid May to mid September.

Large Lace-border *Scopula limboundata*

APRIL	MAY	JUNE	JULY	AUG	SEPT	OCT

Caterpillar Food: A wide variety of woody and herbaceous plants

Nature Notes:

This is our largest and often most distinctive *Scopula* species.

Asian *Scopula* species visit vertebrate eyes, feeding on tears and mucous, perhaps for sodium or protein. At least 30 species of eye-frequenting moths are suspects in the transmission of diseases that affect humans and others that affect livestock.

This is a huge worldwide genus with over 800 species.

Moth: Forewings cream white, with pale yellowish lines, the postmedial with two large bulges near the costa. Most often with much black shading beyond the postmedial line. Hindwings similar. All wings with a sharp dark discal spot.

Caterpillar: Extremely lanky, green or brown, often with a fine dark dorsal line, and with many fine annular rings.

Life Cycle: One to two generations in our area. Pupa winters.

Range: Through much of U.S. and in Canada from Newfoundland to British Columbia.

The Scribbler *Cladara atrolliturata*

APRIL	MAY	JUNE	JULY	AUG	SEPT	OCT

Caterpillar Food: Alders, Paper Birch, maples and willows

Moth: A handsome springtime moth with white forewings crossed by pale green bands and irregular black lines.

Caterpillar: Slender, green, usually unmarked. Spiracles, intersegmental folds and tips of prolegs yellow.

Life Cycle: One generation. Mature caterpillars in June. Pupa winters.

Range: New England to Alabama and north to Minnesota. In Canada from Newfoundland west to central British Columbia.

Nature Notes:

"Scribbler" refers to the complex markings of the forewings.

My records for adults from east central Minnesota, April 15 to May 7.

Perched adults much resemble lichen patches. They show some preference for perching on the pale trunks of Paper Birches.

The Beggar *Eubaphe mendica*

APRIL	MAY	JUNE	JULY	AUG	SEPT	OCT

Caterpillar Food: Violets and possibly maples

Nature Notes:

This is one of the few moths with a chrysalis-type pupa.

"Beggar" refers to the smudged gray patches on the wings, like dirt on a panhandler's coat.

There are 27 known species, six from North America, only one in our area.

Moth: Pale yellow, translucent, with two lines of large, irregular, pale gray blotches corresponding to the antemedial and postmedial lines.

Caterpillar: Very lanky, tan, with many black spots and broken lines.

Life Cycle: Perhaps two generations in our area. Pupa winters.

Range: Much of eastern North America with a few records in northern Idaho and Wyoming. In Canada from Nova Scotia west to northern Alberta, British Columbia.

Brown Bark Carpet *Horisme intestinata*

APRIL	MAY	JUNE	JULY	AUG	SEPT	OCT

Caterpillar Food: Virgin's Bower; possibly other *Clematis* species

Moth: Forewing brown with many dark, wavy parallel lines. Postmedial line deeply scalloped.

Caterpillar: Pale brown with an irregular dark dorsal line with paler edging, widest over thorax. Series of small, dark, setal warts.

Life Cycle: Likely two generations in our area. Pupa winters.

Range: Much of North America; Nova Scotia to northern British Columbia in the north; south to panhandle of Florida and southeast Arizona.

Nature Notes:

The bark-like pattern of the wings is highly cryptic when the moth perches on bark aligned with the vertical furrows.

Of 73 known species, four are North American, only one in our area.

Scallop Shells *Rheumaptera (Hydria) prunivorata/undulata*

APRIL	MAY	JUNE	JULY	AUG	SEPT	OCT

Caterpillar Food: Cherries, especially black cherry

Nature Notes:

While the adult is cryptic and was readily eaten by wild birds in a feeding trial, the striking caterpillars of the Cherry Scallop Shell have not been tested. Perhaps their somewhat bright colors and group presence is a valid warning or just a bluff.

Cherry is also known as Ferguson's Scallop Shell.

These species are only separable by examining internal genitalia or DNA testing.

Moth: Cherry Scallop Shell (*R. prunivorata*) and Scallop Shell (*R. undulata*) are nearly identical. Forewings brown with many fine, scalloped, brown, black and yellow lines, the pattern continued onto the hind wings.

Caterpillar: Dark dorsum with broken pale lines, sides pale cream with dark warts and paler lines. Head red-orange. Feed in groups inside silk-tied clusters of leaves.

Life Cycle: Two generations. Pupa winters.

Range: Much of eastern U.S.; to northern Minnesota, Manitoba and Saskatchewan.

Black Moths *Rheumaptera hastata/subhastata*

APRIL	MAY	JUNE	JULY	AUG	SEPT	OCT

Caterpillar Food: Alders & birches; also blueberries, Sweetfern, Sweetgale

Moth: Spear-marked Black Moth (*R. hastata*) and White-banded Black Moth (*R. subhastata*) are nearly identical. Boldly, complexly and variably black-and-white day-flying moths. Note white "spearhead" mark on forewings.

Caterpillar: Stout, somewhat glossy, often dark brown with broad contrasting longitudinal stripes and a strong subspiracular flange.

Life Cycle: One generation. Pupae winter.

Range: Holarctic; northern U.S., Canada to Iceland to Scandinavia, mainland Europe, Russia, Mongolia and Japan.

Nature Notes:

These two species are only identifiable by internal anatomy. Sometimes considered a species complex—closely related, confusingly similar, but reproductively isolated from each other.

Moths show many pattern variations.

White-banded apparently less common in some areas.

Caterpillars feed inside webbed leaf shelters.

Orange-barred Carpet *Dysstroma hersiliata*

APRIL	MAY	JUNE	JULY	AUG	SEPT	OCT

Caterpillar Food: Currants and gooseberries

Nature Notes:

There may be more species than presently recognized.

Fourteen of 52 known species occur in North America. Some of our species also occur in Europe and the genus is largely holarctic.

Moth: Forewing variably gray to brown, with an even orange bar in the antemedial area and variable orange and white shading beyond the upper postmedial line, which usually has a deep cleft.

Caterpillar: Green with a strong white subdorsal stripe and many minute white spines.

Life Cycle: One generation in our area. Egg winters.

Range: Much of Canada to Alaska, south into northern half of U.S.; New England south into Appalachians, west to Colorado, northern California.

Grapevine Loopers *Eulithis diversilineata/gracilineata*

APRIL	MAY	JUNE	JULY	AUG	SEPT	OCT

Caterpillar Food: Both specialize on grape and woodbine

Moth: Our two Grapevine Looper adults are impossible to tell apart without rearing or dissection.

Caterpillar: Slender, smooth, twig-like or tendril-like; brown in *gracilineata* and green in *diversilineata*.

Life Cycle: One to two generations. Egg winters.

Range: Widely in eastern U.S. and southern Canada; Nova Scotia to central Alberta

Nature Notes:

Grapevine Looper adults have a bizarre perching posture with the abdomen slung forward over the head (inset photo). Contortionism would be a good name for such behavior

A holarctic genus with 27 species, including 14 in North America and nine in our area.

White-striped Black *Trichodezia albovittata*

APRIL	MAY	JUNE	JULY	AUG	SEPT	OCT

Caterpillar Food: Touch-me-nots, willow-herbs and meadow-rues

Nature Notes:

Day-flying, but sometimes comes to light. This moth still has very sensitive "bat detectors" (ears) suggesting that it has become day-flying relatively recently. A good candidate for key-jingling (see "Moth Appreciation and Study").

In flight the boldly contrasting pattern creates an elusive flickering effect.

Moth: Wings black, the forewing crossed by a broad white band.

Caterpillar: Slender, translucent green, with a vague spiracular line, dark edged, especially on thorax, the edging joining across front of head, where darkest. Caterpillar sometimes has a reddish anal plate.

Life Cycle: Likely two generations in our area. Pupa winters.

Range: Mostly northern half of U.S. and Canada to northern Northwest Ontario, central Yukon, Alaska.

Alpine Zenophleps *Zenophleps alpinata*

APRIL	MAY	JUNE	JULY	AUG	SEPT	OCT

Caterpillar Food: Variety of plants; Fireweed, bedstraws, snowberry

Moth: Quite distinctive: forewing cream with pale brown in median, and sometimes basal, areas, especially inside the postmedial line. Antemedial line irregularly convexly curved, postmedial line mostly straight, with a large rounded tooth about midway.

Caterpillar: Beige to yellowish-green with white addorsal lines and a series of darker stripes. Also with small white tubercles darkly ringed at base. To about 1.1 inches.

Life Cycle: One generation. Pupa winters.

Range: Alaska to Manitoba, south to California and Arizona; also with records in far western South Dakota. Apparently also a breeding population in north central Minnesota (see *Nature Notes* sidebar). No historic records were found for Ontario, Minnesota or Wisconsin. But *Zenophleps alpinata* is indeed here and should be watched for in late summer.

Found in boreal and montane conifer forests and shrubby tundra in northern part of its range.

Nature Notes:

Consider this a "Wanted" poster for what appears to be a very locally distributed species in our area (as of 2016, just two known locations in northern Minnesota, but very common in at least one of them. I first encountered them at a light in a pine woods on August 26, 1993 about seven miles east of Itasca State Park near the village of Lake George in Hubbard County. (It then took me 18 years to get an identification!) Sampling since then suggests a robust eastern-outlier breeding population with a single generation flying from mid-August through mid-September. Likely this species will be found at other northern pinewoods locations with further sampling. There is DNA evidence that this species may in fact belong in *Z. lignicolorata* (similarly distributed).

White-ribboned Carpet *Mesoleuca ruficillata*

APRIL	MAY	JUNE	JULY	AUG	SEPT	OCT

Caterpillar Food: Leaves of birches, blackberries (and raspberries?)

Nature Notes:

When I first saw this moth flying (during the day) I was confused by the apparent odd shape defined by the contrast between its dark and light areas—a classic example of disruptive marking.

This is the only *Mesoleuca* species in our three-state area. Five species of *Xanthorhoe* in our region. Most range widely in the North.

Moth: A broad white forewing median band contrasts strongly with a blue-black basal area and with black patches along the costa. Warm brown outside the postmedial line.

Caterpillar: Green with a white spiracular line edged with red at ends and extending broadly (white) onto side of head. Anal plate reddish.

Life Cycle: Likely one generation in our area. Pupa winters.

Range: Forested parts of northern U.S. and southern Canada; Newfoundland nearly Yukon.

Other Carpets...

Sharp-angled Carpet *Euphyia intermediata*

Red Twin-spot *Xanthorhoe ferrugata*

Toothed Brown Carpet *Xanthorhoe lacustrata*

Double-banded Carpet *Spargania magnoliata*

Variable Carpet *Anticlea vasiliata*

The Infant *Archiearis infans*

MARCH	APRIL	MAY	JUNE	JULY	AUG	SEPT

Caterpillar Food: Birch, alder (and their catkins?); possibly poplar, willow

Nature Notes:

A very early-season flyer in the North. Often on the wing by March with the majority of sightings of moths puddling on dirt roads on warm sunny days in April.

Another common name is First-born Geometer.

Specific epithet *infans* is a Latin reference to the adults very early emergence from a pupa in spring.

Caterpillars may feed on catkins before leaves emerge.

Moth: Often rests with wings partially spread to reveal bright orange L-shaped marks on hindwing. Dark brownish-black forewings.

Caterpillar: Green with reddish spiracular spots, white stripes and dots.

Life Cycle: One generation in our area. Pupa winters.

Range: Across our region. A quite northern species that in the East reaches from Manitoba, Ontario, Quebec and Labrador to southern Minnesota, lower Michigan and northern Pennsylvania and New York.

Scarce Infant *Leucobrephos brephoides*

FEB	MARCH	APRIL	MAY	JUNE	JULY	AUG

Caterpillar Food: Paper Birch, Quaking Aspen, Balsam Poplar, alder, willows

Moth: Blackish with wavy white subterminal band. Hindwings white with broad black border. Very fuzzy head.

Caterpillar: Green; wide yellow spiracular stripe.

Life Cycle: One generation in our area. Pupa winters. One of, if not the earliest non-hibernating moths to emerge from a pupa in spring. Sometimes seen when snow still in the woods.

Range: Rarely recorded. Alaska to Labrador and south to Washington, Montana, very northern portions of Minnesota, Wisconsin and Michigan, southern Ontario.

Nature Notes:

Rarely seen. Less than 30 reports on iNaturalist.

Often on the wing when snow still lies deep in the woods.

These photos were taken on March 21 near Big Bog SRA, Minnesota. It was basking in a dirt parking lot surrounded by Black Spruce-Tamarack bog.

Caterpillar likely feeds on catkins of birch, aspen, alder before leaves open.

White-fringed Emerald *Nemoria mimosaria*

APRIL	MAY	JUNE	JULY	AUG	SEPT	OCT

Caterpillar Food: Sweet Fern, Sweet Gale, New Jersey Tea, sumacs

Nature Notes:

With the color green so common in nature, it is curious that more adult moths don't use it to hide from predators. Since white and pale tones often appear green or greenish in forest lighting, perhaps there is less need to produce green pigmentation. Or perhaps it is harder to produce in adults.

The very similar Red-fronted Emerald (*N. rubrifrontaria*) has reddish ringed spots on abdomen; red on head, fringe.

Moth: Pale green with mostly straight white antemedial and postmedial lines that continue onto the hindwings. The abdomen is marked with several white spots.

Caterpillar: Bizarre body outline strongly resembles tattered leaves.

Life Cycle: One generation; Pupa winters.

Range: Eastern U.S. west to Alberta. *N rubrifrontaria* has a more limited range being found from Nova Scotia, New England, New York west to northern Minnesota; a few records south of this area.

Wavy-lined Emerald *Synchlora aerata albolineata*

APRIL	MAY	JUNE	JULY	AUG	SEPT	OCT

Caterpillar Food: Especially flowers of aster family plants

Moth: Pale green with white antemedial and postmedial lines broadly curved and finely wavy. Hindwings similar. White abdominal spots join to form a stripe.

Caterpillar: Mottled with a slanting white line passing through each spiracle. Fragments of food plant debris are attached with silk to a series of projections along the dorsum.

Life Cycle: Likely two generations in our area. Partly grown caterpillar winters.

Range: Most of eastern U.S. and across southern Canada; Northwest Territories to Mexico.

Nature Notes:

Our area hosts the subspecies *albolineata* which tends to be larger and deeper green than the subspecies *aerata* which might just reach the southern edge of our area.

The use of debris to blend in with the food plant is only one of several methods used by emerald moth caterpillars. Others change color or shape depending on the food plant.

Blackberry Looper *Chlorochlamys chloroleucaria*

APRIL	MAY	JUNE	JULY	AUG	SEPT	OCT

Caterpillar Food: Fruits and flowers of raspberries and blackberries

Nature Notes:

Adults fly day and night. They come to lights but perhaps not very often relative to their numbers.

There are 74 known North American species in this subfamily of about 2500 worldwide; six or seven occur in our area.

Chlorochlamys caterpillars show marked color variations—green, pink, yellow—that match their food.

Moth: Wings grayish green, fading to yellowish with age. The cream white antemedial and postmedial lines are nearly straight and continue onto the hindwings. The costal margin is also white. Males have broad feathery antennae.

Caterpillar: Slender green with yellow intersegmental bands. Paired slender horns and the anal plate is sharply pointed. Often a broad reddish middorsal stripe.

Life Cycle: Two generations. Pupa winters.

Range: Most of eastern U.S. and southern Canada; Alberta south to Costa Rica.

Tawny Eupithecia *Eupithecia ravocostaliata*

APRIL	MAY	JUNE	JULY	AUG	SEPT	OCT

Caterpillar Food: Especially willows; also poplars, cherries, viburnums

Moth: A standout among *Eupithecias* for its size and distinctive appearance: forewings long and narrow, variegated in gray, white, and brown, with strong dark shading narrowly along the costal margin. Hindwings much shorter.

Caterpillar: Slender, green, with a strong yellow and red lateral stripe, dorsum with many small white dots.

Life Cycle: One generation. Pupa winters.

Range: Nova Scotia, New England, New York west to Minnesota, Manitoba. In West along Pacific from Baja to British Columbia.

Nature Notes:

Also known as Tawny Pug or Great Variegated Pug.

Most Eupithecias ("pugs")are small to very small, forewings often elongate, pale cream to brown, mostly obscurely marked. Many identifiable only by details of internal reproductive anatomy.

There is a remarkable group of *Eupithecia* in the Hawaiian Islands, whose caterpillars feed on live flies captured with a snapping backward lunge.

Brown-bordered Geometer *Eumacaria madopata*

APRIL	MAY	JUNE	JULY	AUG	SEPT	OCT

Caterpillar Food: Cherries, apples and plums (Rose family)

Nature Notes:

I have seen only three light captures from east central Minnesota (May 26, July 29 and August 21) and have seen the caterpillar once, on apple.

Perched adults resemble skeletonized patches in dead leaves.

Moth: Forewing and hindwing similarly marked, pale gray to postmedial line, contrasting darker brown outside it. Lines and veins darker.

Caterpillar: Pale gray, flushed complexly with reddish tones, anterior two to five abdominal spiracles surrounded by dark patches.

Life Cycle: Possibly a partial second generation in our region. Pupa winters.

Range: Much of U.S. west to Colorado, Idaho, Oregon, and all across southern Canada; only a few records in our three states.

Currant Spanworm Moth *Macaria ribearia*

APRIL	MAY	JUNE	JULY	AUG	SEPT	OCT

Caterpillar Food: Currants and gooseberries

Moth: Translucent pale yellow with diffuse gray postmedial line and gray-washed basal and postmedial areas.

Caterpillar: Strikingly handsome in bold yellow, white and black.

Life Cycle: One generation. Egg winters.

Range: Mostly northern U.S. and southern Canada west to Colorado, Montana, British Columbia; northern sightings from Yukon to Labrador.

Nature Notes:

Though adults can be abundant, the caterpillars are surprisingly easy to miss. I'd seen hundreds of adults before I ever found a caterpillar.

This is one species that may have been hurt by a long-standing, misguided, discontinued, effort to eradicate currants and gooseberries, intermediate hosts of the White Pine Blister Rust.

Barred Angle *Macaria subcessaria*

APRIL	MAY	JUNE	JULY	AUG	SEPT	OCT

Caterpillar Food: Currants and gooseberries

Nature Notes:

Barred Angle is one of the most reliably encountered "angles" in east central Minnesota.

Macaria truncataria is an attractive day-flier of bogs and other habitats where Bearberry and Leatherleaf occur (opposite page).

The Four-spotted Macaria (*Macaria coortaria*) also has four dark spots (none elongated into a bar). Caterpillar feeds on members of the rose family.

Moth: Pale gray-brown, with four dark marks along each forewing costa, one of them a strong bar.

Caterpillar: Green and brown forms, very different from one another; complexly marked.

Life Cycle: One generation. Egg winters.

Range: Much of eastern U.S. and southern edge of Canada; southern Michigan across southern Wisconsin to northern Minnesota and Manitoba.

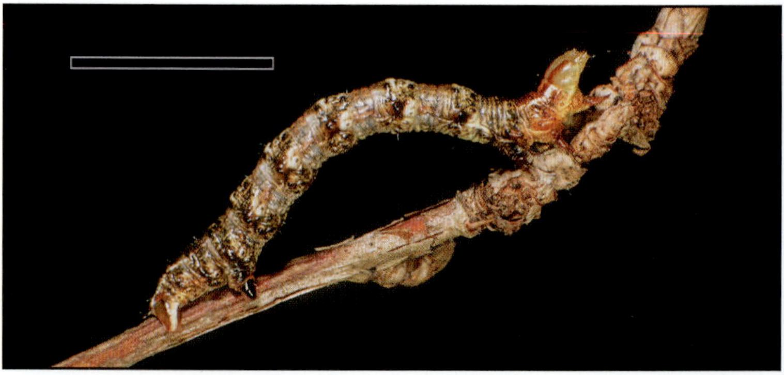

Other Macaria & Digrammia species...

Black-banded Orange
Macaria truncataria

Sulphur Angle
Macaria sulphurea

Four-spotted Macaria
Macaria coortaria

Lesser Maple Spanworm
Macaria pustularia

Common Angle
Macaria aemulataria

Red-headed Inchworm
Macaria bisignata

White Pine Angle
Macaria pinistrobata

Lesser Larch Angle
Macaria oweni

Curve-lined Angle
Digrammia continuata

Yellow-lined Angle
Digrammia mellistrigata

Small Engrailed *Ectropis crepuscularia*

APRIL	MAY	JUNE	JULY	AUG	SEPT	OCT

Caterpillar Food: Variety of broadleaved & coniferous woody plants

Nature Notes:

This is one of the more distinctive "grays," a group that has confounded many a lepidopterist.

Only one of over 100 listed species is known from North America. Forbes (1948) mentioned only "several more species" in the Old World, so some major revision has evidently occurred.

Caterpillar of Tulip-tree Beauty (below) feeds on Pawpaw, Sassafras, Tuliptree and poplars.

Moth: Wings powdery gray, with toothed, blackish lines. Note, especially, a close-set pair of dark "spikes" pointed outward about midway along outside of postmedial line.

Caterpillar: Twig-like. Complexly mottled. Red-brown with an enlarged thorax, often a white slash above and along front of first proleg and a dark **V** over eighth abdominal segment.

Life Cycle: Two generations. Pupa winters.

Range: Holarctic; North America to Russia, Japan. Tulip-tree Beauty only to southern Lower Michigan in our region.

Tulip-tree Beauty *Epimecis hortaria*

Peppered Moth *Biston betularia*

APRIL	MAY	JUNE	JULY	AUG	SEPT	OCT

Caterpillar Food: Many plants but especially Paper Birch and willows

Moth: Forewing long, white, heavily and evenly dotted with black, resulting in overall appearance of dark or lighter gray.

Caterpillar: Large, with a deeply cleft head. Fifth abdominal segment with a pair of warts above the spiracles. Lateral fringe of subventral setae between prolegs. Spiracles often orange.

Life Cycle: Apparently one extended generation in our region. Pupa winters.

Range: Holarctic; across North America to England, mainland Europe, Russia, China, Japan.

Nature Notes:

This species was the subject of a classic study of "industrial melanism" by H. B. D. Kettlewell in England in the 1950s. Polluted areas with few pale lichens on tree trunks appeared to favor an increase in the dark form since they were harder for birds to find than the lighter "typical" forms. The study has recently generated much controversy and clearly begs refinement.

Linden Looper *Erannis tiliaria*

MAY	JUNE	JULY	AUG	SEPT	OCT	NOV

Caterpillar Food: Basswood (Linden), variety of broadleaved trees, shrubs

Nature Notes:

One of the commonest moths at porch lights in late autumn. My Minnesota records are mostly mid to late October.

Caterpillars are sometimes numerous enough to widely defoliate trees in spring and early summer.

Males have large wings for their body size and can fly with their bodies below freezing.

Sometimes called Winter Moth or Basswood Looper.

Moth: Male forewings yellow to pale brown, with thin, curved, brown antemedial and postmedial lines. Females are essentially wingless with mottled black and white bodies and legs.

Caterpillar: Warm brown back separated from bright yellow sides by a dark subdorsal line; belly white. Head brown, often unmarked. Spiracles ringed with black. Often hold anterior abdomen arched.

Life Cycle: One generation. Egg winters.

Range: New England through our region to Northwest Territories; south to Texas, Florida.

The Half-wing *Phigalia titea*

MARCH	APRIL	MAY	JUNE	JULY	AUG	SEPT

Caterpillar Food: A wide range of broad-leaved woody plants

Moth: Males with pale gray wings with wavy double antemedial and postmedial lines and a straight medial line. Females have only tiny nubs for wings.

Caterpillar: Pale gray with numerous, thin, broken stripes, orange tints especially around the spiracles and setae borne from black warts. Head has many black spots.

Life Cycle: One generation. Pupa winters.

Range: Much of eastern U.S. and southern Canada; Nova Scotia to Alberta. South to southeast Arizona, Texas, central Florida.

Nature Notes:

Males are light relative to their wing size and able to fly at very low temperatures without shivering to warm their flight muscles.

This species has a melanic (dark) form which, in a study of perching behavior, preferred white birch trunks over more neutral-colored trunks.

Small Phigalia *Phigalia strigataria*

MARCH	APRIL	MAY	JUNE	JULY	AUG	SEPT

Caterpillar Food: A wide range of broad-leaved woody plants

Nature Notes:

Early-season moths avoid much predation by birds and bats.

If necessary, the young caterpillars can drift on silk strands in search of favorable food, compensating for their flightless mothers.

Moth: The forewing markings are weaker than in The Half-wing (*Phigalia titea*) (on previous page). Flightless females with tiny wings.

Caterpillar: A mix of yellow and brown with strong dark warts on the second and third abdominal segments.

Life Cycle: One generation. Pupa winters.

Range: Much of eastern U.S. and southeast Canada; Quebec to southern Manitoba. Minnesota is northwest range limit in the U.S.; south to Florida, Texas, Mexico City.

Stout Spanworm *Lycia ursaria*

APRIL	MAY	JUNE	JULY	AUG	SEPT	OCT

Caterpillar Food: Many broadleaved woody plants

Moth: Medium-sized, forewing gray, with three black lines and a white subterminal line. Very hairy. Females have large wings, but do not fly.

Caterpillar: Pinkish, with many fine, wavy, black stripes. True legs and head reddish. Strong yellow subdorsal and lateral warts.

Life Cycle: One generation. Mature caterpillars mid to late summer. My earliest (very small) caterpillar from east central Minnesota was found on May 31. Pupa winters.

Range: Northern one-third of U.S. to northern Quebec, central Alaska.

Nature Notes:

The caterpillars sometimes grow very slowly, but a quarter-inch caterpillar I found on ash on May 31 had reached full size (2.25 inches) by June 19.

The large-winged females cannot fly. Production of mature eggs is accompanied by expansion of the ovaries into the thorax, displacing normal flight muscles.

Yellow-dusted Cream *Cabera erythemaria*

APRIL	MAY	JUNE	JULY	AUG	SEPT	OCT

Caterpillar Food: Especially willows; also poplars

Nature Notes:

The Pink-striped Willow Spanworm Moth (*C. variolaria*), our other common species, is white with yellow-brown on the front of its head and forelegs. It flies mid May to early September in Wisconsin. Its caterpillar is perhaps indistinguishable from that of *erythemaria* and eats the same plants.

Moth: Wings cream white with yellowish dusting and faint, mostly parallel, yellowish-brown antemedial, median and postmedial lines, the latter two extending onto the hindwings.

Caterpillar: Slender, pale green or brown, with irregular white stripes; a dark stripe along side of head onto thorax and along sides of prolegs.

Life Cycle: Likely one extended generation in our area. Pupa winters.

Range: Much of northern U.S. and southern Canada; Newfoundland to Alaska.

Fall Cankerworm Moth *Alsophila pometaria*

MAY	JUNE	JULY	AUG	SEPT	OCT	NOV

Caterpillar Food: New foliage of many broadleaved woody plants

Moth: A small gray moth with the postmedial line sharply inset below the forewing costa. Females (inset photo) only have wing nubs.

Caterpillar: Color highly variable, from pale green to black. The half-sized third pair of prolegs on fifth abdominal segment confirms identification.

Life Cycle: One generation. Eggs winter in tight clusters on twigs or trunks. Caterpillars eclose in early spring and pupate in May or June.

Range: Widespread across the U.S. and southern Canada; Newfoundland to Alberta.

Nature Notes:

Males are able to fly at temperatures down to freezing to avoid bat predation.

My latest date for East Central Minnesota is November 9th!

Caterpillars can cause widespread defoliation.

Flightless females are often found on the sides of buildings near woody vegetation, or trunks of trees at night.

Pale Beauty *Campaea perlata*

APRIL	MAY	JUNE	JULY	AUG	SEPT	OCT

Caterpillar Food: Birch, White Spruce, Tamarack, blueberry & cranberry

Nature Notes:

Abundance can fluctuate markedly year to year.

The pale green adults tend to perch pressed against the undersides of living leaves where they are largely invisible, sheltered from direct sun and rain and more energetically costly for birds to hunt.

The considerable sexual size difference likely reflects the need for females to carry eggs.

Moth: A medium-sized, pale green beauty! Females larger than males.

Caterpillar: Neutral shades of green through red, with a fringe of pale hairs along the lower margin and a third pair of smaller prolegs on the fifth abdominal segment.

Life Cycle: Two generations. Caterpillars winter partly grown, likely fully exposed to the elements.

Range: Much of North America; Florida to southern California; Newfoundland to Hudson Bay and west to Yukon and central Alaska.

Ruddy Metarranthis *Metarranthis duaria*

APRIL	MAY	JUNE	JULY	AUG	SEPT	OCT

Caterpillar Food: Especially favor blueberries and cherries

Moth: A highly variable species with broad, pointed forewings angled at the outer margin. Shades of yellowish or reddish gray with curved antemedial line and bent postmedial line which continues onto the hindwing. Conspicuous discal spots on the fore- and hindwings.

Caterpillar: Brown, gray or reddish with humped eighth abdominal segment. Small headed.

Life Cycle: Likely one generation in our area. Pupa winters.

Range: Much of the eastern U.S. and Pacific Northwest; across southern Canada from Newfoundland to northern British Columbia.

Nature Notes:

Ruddy Metarranthis is the most common species in this genus.

Many *Metarranthis* species are strictly diurnal and rarely found at lights. Others fly day and night and arrive more often at lights.

Adults perch on fallen leaves.

All 13 species are North American; about five species reach our area.

Scallop Moth *Cepphis armataria*

APRIL	MAY	JUNE	JULY	AUG	SEPT	OCT

Caterpillar Food: Many broadleaved woody plants

Nature Notes:

Apparently quite uncommon.

My seven Minnesota records all from June.

The caterpillars are remarkably cryptic. I found the group below hanging head-down amidst their feeding damage and silk tethers, looking very much like dead leaf fragments in a spider web. When disturbed they swayed side to side.

Moth: All wings deeply scalloped, warm brown with darker, purplish lines; postmedial line double. Perched on leaf litter in which they much resemble dead leaves.

Caterpillar: Stout, mottled brown, anterior abdominal segments swelled dorsally and laterally. Large, irregular white wedge on side of fourth through sixth abdominal segments. Head small.

Life Cycle: Likely one brood in our area. Pupa winters.

Range: Restricted to northeastern U.S. and adjacent Canada; Nova Scotia to Manitoba.

Northern Thorn *Selenia alciphearia*

APRIL	MAY	JUNE	JULY	AUG	SEPT	OCT

Caterpillar Food: Willows and a variety of other broadleaved woody plants

Moth: Stout, medium large, with rusty tan to brown angled forewings. White shading of the undersides of the hindwings is mostly inside the quite straight double postmedial line.

Caterpillar: Stout, very twig-like; especially thick just ahead of the front prolegs.

Life Cycle: Likely one generation in our area. Pupa winters.

Range: All across forested northern U.S. (New England, Appalachians, our region, Pacific Northwest) and southern Canada; Newfoundland to central Alaska.

Nature Notes:

Kent's Geometer (*S. kentaria*) flies May to late July (inset photo above). It is similar but is yellower and has white shading on the wing undersides outside the wavier postmedial lines.

Adults perch with wings held together over their backs like butterflies, an uncommon posture in moths.

Also known as Northern Selenia or Brown-tipped Thorn.

Straight-lined Plagodis *Plagodis phlogosaria*

APRIL	MAY	JUNE	JULY	AUG	SEPT	OCT

Caterpillar Food: Variety of broadleaved trees and shrubs

Nature Notes:

Often common at lights in May.

Caterpillars are very twig-like.

The Purple Plagodis (*P. kuetzingi*) is a specialist on ash.

Some *Plagodis* adults appear more cryptic than others. Whether the brighter, bolder ones are chemically defended is unknown.

Moth: *Plagodis* moths are brown, purple and yellow with angled outer forewing margins. Postmedial lines usually strong, sometimes strongly shaded, sometimes dividing dark outer from light inner areas. Some *Plagodis* species have distinct spring and summer forms.

Caterpillar: Dorsally humped fifth abdominal segment. Second thoracic segment enlarged and the markings twig-like.

Life Cycle: Two generations. Pupa winters.

Range: Five broad-ranging species found in our three-state region.

Other Plagodis...

Lemon Plagodis

Plagodis serinaria

91a-1185

Purple Plagodis

Plagodis kuetzingi

91a-1186

Fervid Plagodis

Plagodis fervidaria

91a-1189

Hollow-spotted Plagodis

Plagodis alcoolaria

91a-1190

Dark Metanema *Metanema determinata*

APRIL	MAY	JUNE	JULY	AUG	SEPT	OCT

Caterpillar Food: Especially willows, also aspens and ash

Nature Notes:

The pretty Pale Metanema (*M. inatomaria*) [inset photo] has thin yellow antemedial and postmedial lines and a red-brown discal spot. Outer margins strongly angled. Flies mid May to mid August.

Common at lights.

The caterpillars are well hidden when resting on twigs or trunks.

Moth: Dark gray with bold lines, the postmedial line double. Outer forewing margin strongly angled.

Caterpillar: Somewhat flattened, with a complex pattern of brown and gray, including a series of large, pale dorsal areas, subtler and less triangular than in the Pale Metanema. Browner than Pale Metanema.

Life Cycle: Two generations. Pupa winters.

Range: New England, Appalachians south to North Carolina; west to Colorado, Montana. In Canada from Newfoundland to Yukon.

Common Lytrosis *Lytrosis unitaria*

APRIL	MAY	JUNE	JULY	AUG	SEPT	OCT

Caterpillar Food: Especially Sugar Maple and hawthorns

Moth: Outer margins of wings scalloped. Pale gray, yellow-brown and brown, with thin black postmedial lines. Female larger, with more pale gray. All wings similarly patterned.

Caterpillar: Big, twig-like, generally pale, with many dark markings and warts. First abdominal segment with a pair of dark, fused, subdorsal swellings. Fifth abdominal with a pair of elongate, posteriorly curved, fleshy horns.

Life Cycle: One generation.

Range: Most of eastern U.S.; across our region to Canadian border.

Nature Notes:

This "wood-grained" moth perches with all wings exposed and aligned to match the vertical furrows of bark. The abdomen is usually held slightly upward to obscure the shadow line of the upper hindwing.

The caterpillars closely resemble twigs. A half-grown one I found on hackberry in April regurgitated its gut contents when first discovered.

Johnson's Euchlaena *Euchlaena johnsonaria*

APRIL	MAY	JUNE	JULY	AUG	SEPT	OCT

Caterpillar Food: Variety of broadleaved woody & herbaceous plants

Nature Notes:

While some species are quite attractive, even those resemble dead leaves. Despite this, a small feeding trial including two species offered to wild birds indicated they may have some chemical defense. Markings and colors vary and time will tell how many species there truly are; some have turned out to be just seasonal forms.

Moth: *Euchlaena* species are medium-sized, cryptic moths that tend to have scalloped and/or angled outer wing margins.

Caterpillar: Drab, twig-like, often with dorsal knobs on posterior abdominal segments.

Life Cycle: Winter as partly-grown caterpillars.

Range: Widely in North America, with about ten species in our three-state region. *E. amoenaria* included based on one Minnesota record.

The Saw-wing

Euchlaena serrata

Obtuse Euchlaena

Euchlaena obtusaria

Other Euchlaena...

Deep Yellow Euchlaena

Euchlaena amoenaria

Ochre Euchlaena

Euchlaena marginaria

Mottled Euchlaena

Euchlaena tigrinaria

Least-marked Euchlaena

Euchlaena serrata

Crocus Geometers *Xanthotype sospeta/urticaria*

APRIL	MAY	JUNE	JULY	AUG	SEPT	OCT

Caterpillar Food: Many broadleaved plants; Poison Ivy

Nature Notes:

Five North American *Xanthotype* species but only two commonly in our region – *X. sospeta* (Crocus Geometer) and *X. urticaria* (False Crocus Geometer).

Somewhat day-active, but also come readily to light.

I have twice seen the caterpillars feeding on Poison Ivy.

Moth: Pale to bright yellow, variably marked with pinkish brown blotches or dusting. Crocus Geometer (*X. sospeta*) is said to be paler yellow and less marked with brown (inset photo?), but the species can be known with certainty only by internal reproductive anatomy.

Caterpillar: Long, slender, pale green or brown, with a white spiracular stripe.

Life Cycle: Likely two generations in our area. Partly grown caterpillar winters.

Range: Much of northeastern U.S. and southern Canada, but identification difficult.

Morrison's Pero *Pero morrisonaria*

APRIL	MAY	JUNE	JULY	AUG	SEPT	OCT

Caterpillar Food: Conifers. Reports from others need confirmation

Moth: Sharp, wavy postmedial line divides a contrastingly dark median area from the subterminal area. Light brown in both sexes and variably dark-speckled. Outer wing margins scalloped.

Caterpillar: Brown, vaguely and finely striped. Top of head squared, with an anterior projecting lobe on each side.

Life Cycle: Two generations in most of range. Pupa winters in a thin cocoon in leaf litter.

Range: Occurs widely across the U.S. and southern Canada; south to Colombia, Brazil.

Nature Notes:

Peros perch with the front edge of the forewings folded, remarkably resembling a curled dead leaf. *Pero* is Greek for "maimed" or "mutilated," likely in reference to this posture.

Honest Pero (*P. honestaria*) and Hubner's Pero (*P. ancetaria*) also in our area, are less speckled and reported to feed on broadleaved woody plants, though records from conifers and forbs exist.

Sharp-lined Yellow *Sicya macularia*

APRIL	MAY	JUNE	JULY	AUG	SEPT	OCT

Caterpillar Food: Many plants; especially aspens, willows and alders

Nature Notes:

Eggs are black and attached on their sides.

The pupa is metallic gold.

Adults perch atop living leaves with their wings sharply tented and their heads held to the surface, in which posture they resemble fallen yellow leaves. It is unknown whether the coloration is cryptic or advertises chemical defense.

Moth: Forewing angled, bright yellow, brown shading beyond postmedial line, more even in the males.

Caterpillar: Drab brown and green gray, with irregular finger-like midline protuberances and an oblique white line along outside edge of front proleg.

Life Cycle: One extended generation in our area. Egg winters.

Range: All across North America (absent from Deep South of U.S.); from northern Yukon, central Alaska south to Mexico.

Northern Pine Looper *Caripeta piniata*

APRIL	MAY	JUNE	JULY	AUG	SEPT	OCT

Caterpillar Food: Especially on pines

Moth: Forewings orange-brown. Strong antemedial and postmedial lines accented with white and distinct white discal spots.

Caterpillar: Variegated in brown, red-brown or gray. Lack prominent warts but have an overall rough texture suggesting a conifer twig, due partly to low ridges that connect pairs of dorsal setae.

Life Cycle: One generation. Grown caterpillars common in late summer/fall. Pupa winters.

Range: Restricted to northeastern U.S. and adjacent Canada; northwest range limit in Minnesota, northwest Ontario.

Nature Notes:

Caterpillars are best found with a beating tray (abrupt shaking works well and damages vegetation less) in late summer and fall.

Gray Spruce Looper (*C. divisata*) (below) flies from late June to early August. Its caterpillar feeds on Eastern Hemlock, spruces, firs and Tamarack.

Brown Pine Looper
Caripeta angustoriata

Gray Spruce Looper
Caripeta divisata

Oak Besma *Besma quercivoraria*

APRIL	MAY	JUNE	JULY	AUG	SEPT	OCT

Caterpillar Food: Variety of woody plants, including conifers

Nature Notes:

The Straw Besma (*B. endropiaria*) flies June to mid July and feeds on maples, birches and oaks. Adults are paler, cream-colored, with pale brown wavy lines and dusting. The caterpillar much resembles a reddish twig. Both of these caterpillars are prime examples of what was dubbed "vegetable disguise" by Alfred Russell Wallace, in a more colorful age of science.

Moth: Variable and sexually dimorphic, wings pale yellow, dusted with pale brown, especially on veins. Antemedial and postmedial lines usually a contrasting darker brown. Outer wing margins angled, especially in females.

Caterpillar: Slender, pale, twig-like, with darker, reddish, bud-like swellings on thorax and variously on first, fifth, sixth and eighth abdominal segments.

Life Cycle: Two generations. Pupa winters.

Range: Eastern U.S. and adjacent Canada; also Pacific Northwest south to Honduras.

Hemlock Looper *Lambdina fiscellaria*

APRIL	MAY	JUNE	JULY	AUG	SEPT	OCT

Caterpillar Food: Conifers (sometimes defoliating northern forests)

Moth: Cream to gray with sharp antemedial and postmedial lines. Sometimes has a sharply bent postmedial line and sometimes a darker-shaded median area.

Caterpillar: Boldly striped with black, white, gray and often rusty brown. Head has two pairs of bold black round spots on each side.

Life Cycle: One generation. Egg winters.

Range: Much of the U.S. and all across southern Canada. In the West from northern Alberta, British Columbia to the Pacific Northwest; south to Costa Rica.

Nature Notes:

The taxonomy of this genus is unclear; perhaps other species are yet unrecognized. Photography of caterpillars and careful documentation of preserved adult specimens could help resolve the mystery, as might DNA analysis.

Chain-dotted Geometer *Cingilia catenaria*

APRIL	MAY	JUNE	JULY	AUG	SEPT	OCT

Caterpillar Food: Goldenrod, blueberry, alder, willow, maple, oak, pine

Nature Notes:

Found in bogs and sedge meadows. Caterpillars have been noted feeding on leaves of Bog Buckbean and species of blueberry.

Cingilia is a monotypic genus.

Also called Chain-spotted Geometer.

Caterpillars hang completely straight from a branch, and do a good job of resembling a twig.

Moth: White wings with zigzag median and submedial bands and distinctive black-dotted terminal border ("chain-dotted"). Orange head and "shoulders."

Caterpillar: Pale yellow with longitudinal black and white stripes. Boldly marked with white spots, each sandwiched by black spots.

Life Cycle: One generation. Larvae emerge in June and pupate in August. Egg winters.

Range: Maryland to New England and west to our region; Nova Scotia to Alberta.

False Hemlock Looper *Nepytia canosaria*

APRIL	MAY	JUNE	JULY	AUG	SEPT	OCT

Caterpillar Food: Various conifers

Moth: Pale to dark gray, with dark, white-edged, sharply-toothed antemedial and post-medial lines and distinct dark reniform spots.

Caterpillar: Boldly striped in various colors, including rusty-orange, with a strong yellow lateral stripe and strongly dark-dotted head.

Life Cycle: One generation. Egg winters.

Range: Much of eastern North America. Ranges in the North from Nova Scotia to Northwest Territories in Canada; south to Louisiana, Florida.

Nature Notes:

Bright caterpillar colors and bold markings suggest chemical defense. Even the pupa is brightly colored and visible through the walls of the thin cocoon. But palatability to birds is untested.

The genus needs study as some of the populations and species seem enigmatic. Apparently all 12 or 13 "known" species occur only in North America.

Maple Spanworm *Ennomos magnaria*

MAY	JUNE	JULY	AUG	SEPT	OCT	NOV

Caterpillar Food: Many broadleaved woody plants

Nature Notes:

The caterpillars are superb examples of "vegetable disguise," complete with "buds" and "bud scale scars." The adults resemble shriveled yellow leaves.

Three of 18 described species occur in North America, including two in our region; likely a holarctic genus.

Moth: Wings bright yellow-orange, deeply and unevenly scalloped, speckled with dark brown. Females larger than males.

Caterpillar: Very large, knobby, twig-like, green to brown, with paired, dark, dorsal swellings over second and fifth abdominal segments.

Life Cycle: One generation. Mature caterpillars from mid to late summer. Egg winters.

Range: Much of North America; Newfoundland to Northwest Territories and south to California, New Mexico, Florida.

Snowy Geometer *Eugonobapta nivosaria*

APRIL	MAY	JUNE	JULY	AUG	SEPT	OCT

Caterpillar Food: Basswood, maples, cherries, dogwoods, meadow-rue

Moth: Snowy white; hindwing pointed on lower outer edge.

Caterpillar: Pale green or brown, translucent, paler at intersegmental bands.

Life Cycle: Likely a partial second generation in our area. Egg winters.

Range: Much of eastern U.S. and southern Canada; Nova Scotia to Saskatchewan and south to Oklahoma, Georgia.

Nature Notes:

Could be confused with the Elm Spanworm Moth (*Ennomos subsignaria*) which is a bit larger, duller white, with angled outer *forewing* margins. It flies late June to early September in Wisconsin.

This is the only known species in the genus.

Yellow Slant-line *Tetracis crocallata*

APRIL	MAY	JUNE	JULY	AUG	SEPT	OCT

Caterpillar Food: Willows, alders, sumacs and Red Elderberry

Nature Notes:

In a feeding trial, Yellow Slant-lines were shunned by wild native birds, indicating possible chemical defense.

White Slant-line's (*T. cachexiata*) (inset above) wings are cream white with an orange postmedial line that meets the costal margin near the apex. Caterpillar favors Paper Birch and Tamarack.

Moth: Orange-yellow wings with angled outer margins, small dark discal spots and no antemedial line. Forewings crossed from tip to inner margin by a strong brown postmedial line.

Caterpillar: Twig like, red-brown, with a small flattened head and large subdorsal warts on the mesothorax.

Life Cycle: One generation. Pupa winters.

Range: Eastern U.S. and southern Canada; Nova Scotia to Alberta, south to Florida.

Curve-toothed Geometer *Eutrapela clemataria*

APRIL	MAY	JUNE	JULY	AUG	SEPT	OCT

Caterpillar Food: Many broadleaved and coniferous woody plants

Moth: Wings pale brown with lightly scalloped margins. Postmedial line thin, pale, lightly curved, angled sharply back near costa. Males smaller than females.

Caterpillar: Brown, twig-like, with a raised collar with red lateral extensions over thorax, strongly raised paired lobes over fourth abdominal segment and a smaller pair over eighth.

Life Cycle: One generation in our area. Pupa winters.

Range: Most of eastern U.S. and southern Canada; south to Texas, Florida.

Nature Notes:

Adults perched in the understory or on leaf litter strongly match dead leaves.

Adults resemble the Large Maple Spanworm (page 124), but in that species the postmedial line forms a rounded curve near the costa while in the Curve-toothed Geometer it bends very sharply.

Large Maple Spanworm *Prochoerodes lineola*

APRIL	MAY	JUNE	JULY	AUG	SEPT	OCT

Caterpillar Food: Oaks, maples, aspens, birches, fir & N. White Cedar

Nature Notes:

Apparently there are many close relatives (in this or related genera?) in tropical America. There are seven known North American species and 24 in all.

Formerly known as *P. transversata*.

variation

Moth: Quite variable; forewings straw yellow to brown, wavy antemedial line and mostly straight postmedial line arched outward to below apex.

Caterpillar: Highly variable. Enlarged paired subdorsal warts on fourth and eighth abdominal segments and swollen second thoracic segment. Usually pale to reddish brown.

Life Cycle: Likely one extended generation. Egg winters.

Range: Eastern U.S. and adjacent Canada; Newfoundland to Northwest Territories.

Horned Spanworm *Nematocampa resistaria*

APRIL	MAY	JUNE	JULY	AUG	SEPT	OCT

Caterpillar Food: Many plants; sometimes common on herbaceous plants

Moth: Male smaller, pale yellow, female cream white, both with brown veins and lines. Brown shading of double postmedial line heavier and outer wing margin more sharply angled in female.

Caterpillar: Complexly mottled black, tan and white, but easily recognized by paired, curled, extendable tentacles on second and third abdominal segments. They resemble tattered pieces of dead leaf.

Life Cycle: Perhaps a partial second generation in our area. Egg winters.

Range: Much of the U.S.; Newfoundland, Alberta south to Florida, Ecuador, Brazil.

Nature Notes:

Adults resemble dead leaves, veins and all, but sometimes perch under live leaves, where they resemble dead patches (necroses). To birds expending energy and time to search under fluttering, back-lit, living leaves, such moth is perhaps less rewarding prey than when resting upon dead leaf litter, where it is also very cryptic.

Prominents
Family Notodontidae

Adult feeding varies, with most tropical species having developed mouthparts, while most northern species do not. The metathoracic tympanal hearing organs are uniquely recessed and face ventrally. Each is supplied by one sensory neuron and is generally less sensitive compared with those of noctuids. The common family name refers to the erect scale tufts present on the inner margin of the forewing in the subfamily Notodontinae.

Moths

Adults tend to be drab and cryptic, often obscurely marked, making them hard for birds to find and lepidopterists to identify. Their perching postures often remarkably enhance their camouflage. In many species the wings are rolled tubelike and held out away from a twig to which the head is closely pressed, often hidden between the extended hairy forelegs. Thus perched, they resemble broken off twigs. Others, such as Closteras, strongly resemble dead leaves. Others cloak their wings around a twig or hold them tented.

Caterpillars

Caterpillars are highly diverse. Some (or all?) are sensitive to low-frequency sound through their setae. Many have remarkable defenses, such as the ability to squirt streams of acid from ventral prothoracic "cervical" glands or extrude filaments that exude volatile chemicals from highly modified hind prolegs. The caterpillars feed mostly on woody rather than herbaceous plants.

Diversity (Species Richness/Range)

A large family of over 3200 species worldwide, especially diverse in the American tropics (over 1300 species) and including 136 in North America, about 50 in our area. Eight subfamilies are currently recognized, all occur in North America, five in our area.

Sigmoid Prominent *Clostera albosigma*

APRIL	MAY	JUNE	JULY	AUG	SEPT	OCT

Caterpillar Food: Aspens & willows; also alders, birches, maples & elms

Moth: This species is by far the most common of the five species in our area. All brown or gray crossed by complex patterns of pale wavy lines shaded with dark (most conspicuous at the costa).

Caterpillar: More diverse than the adults, complexly striped, with many pale hairs of short to moderate length and shiny black heads.

Life Cycle: Possibly a partial second generation in the longer-flying species. Pupa winters.

Range: Holarctic; to Russia, China, Korea, Japan. Across North America; Newfoundland to central Alaska in the North; south to Texas.

Nature Notes:

Perched adults uncannily suggest the effect of light skimming a crinkled leaf.

Only North American notodontid genus whose caterpillars do not squirt defensive streams of acid.

Males have been seen drinking copiously at puddles while squirting water from the rear, probably to gather sodium, a scarce nutrient for terrestrial herbivores.

Black-rimmed Prominent *Pheosia rimosa*

APRIL	MAY	JUNE	JULY	AUG	SEPT	OCT

Caterpillar Food: Poplars and willows

Nature Notes:

Adult's perching posture and coloration may obscure its true outline, making it harder for predators to recognize (see inset photo).

Caterpillars feed carefully, eating all of a leaf before moving on, minimizing visual signs of their presence.

The caterpillars are sometimes called "mirror-backed" because of their high gloss.

Moth: Forewings mostly white, with black edging along costa and along inner margin. Hind wings white, with black at anal angle. Females larger than males.

Caterpillar: Usually either pinkish gray or pale green, very shiny, with a black horn on eighth abdominal segment. Spiracles black, ringed with white.

Life Cycle: Likely a partial second generation in our area. Pupa winters.

Range: Holarctic. Newfoundland to central Alaska; south to southeast Arizona, Tennessee.

Elegant Prominent *Pheosidea elegans*

APRIL	MAY	JUNE	JULY	AUG	SEPT	OCT

Caterpillar Food: Poplars; possibly only Quaking Aspen

Moth: Forewings pale gray, darker along costal margin, with a white basal streak and dark streaks along veins. Usual lines absent. Brown scale tuft on inner margin. Females larger than males.

Caterpillar: Shiny, twiglike, gray, reddish, green or brown, with humped second and eighth abdominal segments. True legs and mandibles often red.

Life Cycle: Likely one generation in our area. Pupa winters.

Range: Northern half of the U.S.; Newfoundland to central British Columbia.

Nature Notes:

This is a monotypic genus in North America.

Formerly *Odontosia elegans*.

Northern Finned Prominent *Notodonta torva*

APRIL	MAY	JUNE	JULY	AUG	SEPT	OCT

Caterpillar Food: Poplars and willows

Nature Notes:

The Finned-willow Prominent (*N. scitipennis*) is paler gray, with much warm brown shading basally and along the outer margin, a basal black dash and an even black terminal line.

I have often seen this species at lights in east central Minnesota, but have encountered *N. scitipennis* only once.

A small holarctic genus with three North American species.

Moth: Dark gray, with lines light and dark, postmedial sharply bent below costa. The reniform spot is a dark bar outlined in white.

Caterpillar: Pale gray, with fleshy fin-like projections over second and third abdominal segments and a large hump on the eighth.

Life Cycle: One generation. Pupa winters.

Range: Holarctic; across Europe to Russia, China, South Korea, Japan. Restricted to Northeastern U.S. (New England to Minnesota, south to West Virginia); in Canada from Newfoundland to British Columbia.

Double-toothed Prominent *Nerice bidentata*

APRIL	MAY	JUNE	JULY	AUG	SEPT	OCT

Caterpillar Food: Elms

Moth: Double-toothed blackish band edged with white divides forewing into grayish brown lower half and light to dark brown upper half.

Caterpillar: Green and pale whitish, with coarsely saw-toothed dorsal profile.

Life Cycle: In our area perhaps a partial second generation. Pupa winters.

Range: All of eastern U.S. and southern Canada; Nova Scotia to Saskatchewan.

Nature Notes:

In profile the caterpillar suggests the jagged edge of a partly eaten elm leaf and in feeding position it blends with the void created in the leaf.

Because of its preference for elms and the vulnerability of native elms to Dutch elm disease, this species is a conservation concern.

Adult's bold markings obscure its profile, misleading predator eyes.

Common Gluphisia *Gluphisia septentrionis*

APRIL	MAY	JUNE	JULY	AUG	SEPT	OCT

Caterpillar Food: Poplars

Nature Notes:

While the majority of northern notodontids do not feed, male Common Gluphisias can drink from a puddle for hours while rhythmically squirting water from the rear, to a distance of over a foot. They are gathering sodium, an element in especially low supply in aspen foliage. The sodium is passed to females at mating and then to the eggs.

Moth: Raised shiny black scales in the median area and very faint lines. Four-spotted has distinguishing yellow forewing spots (see inset).

Caterpillar: Green to blue-green, mostly smooth, translucent. Strong yellow subdorsal lines and highly variable red and yellow patches dorsally (sometimes none; see inset photo).

Life Cycle: Likely at least a partial second generation; one generation in the other *Gluphisia* species. Pupa winters.

Range: Widely across the U.S.; south to Texas; Newfoundland to southeast Alaska.

Black-etched Prominent *Cerura scitiscripta*

APRIL	MAY	JUNE	JULY	AUG	SEPT	OCT

Caterpillar Food: Aspen and willow, also cherry

Moth: Forewings white, with sharp, black, double, zigzag lines. Some yellowish shading inside double lines and black streaks along veins.

Caterpillar: Bright green, with long, dark, paired "tails," a strongly humped first abdominal segment, strong white subdorsal and subspiracular stripes and speckling and white spiracles ringed with black.

Life Cycle: Two generations in much of its range, but perhaps not here. Pupa winters.

Range: Most of eastern U.S. and southern Canada; Nova Scotia to Saskatchewan.

Nature Notes:

Caterpillars, when disturbed, throw their hind-quarters over their backs while extruding bright red filaments which emit a volatile chemical presumed to deter predators. Since this can be evoked by certain frequencies of sound it has been surmised that it may be a response to flying insect predators.

Apparently rare or local, or perhaps just not easily trapped with light.

White Furcula *Furcula borealis*

APRIL	MAY	JUNE	JULY	AUG	SEPT	OCT

Caterpillar Food: Prefers cherries; also aspen and willows

Nature Notes:

Caterpillars much resemble blemished leaves. When disturbed (try humming, buzzing or coughing near them) they throw their hind quarters forward over their backs while spreading the tentacle-like hind prolegs and extruding bright filaments from them which release a volatile chemical.

Most *Furcula* caterpillars favor aspen and willows.

Four *Furcula* species in our three-state region.

Moth: Adult *Furcula* species differ subtly, all having basal, subterminal and terminal lines represented by rows of dark dots and all having median and upper subterminal areas contrastingly dark gray.

Caterpillar: Pale yellowish to green, with a dark "saddle" of brown. Hind prolegs highly modified into slender, paired stemapoda which are usually held together behind.

Life Cycle: Pupa winters in spindle-shaped cocoon of chewed bark glued to twigs with silk.

Range: All widely in eastern North America.

Other Furculas...

Gray Furcula *Furcula cinerea*

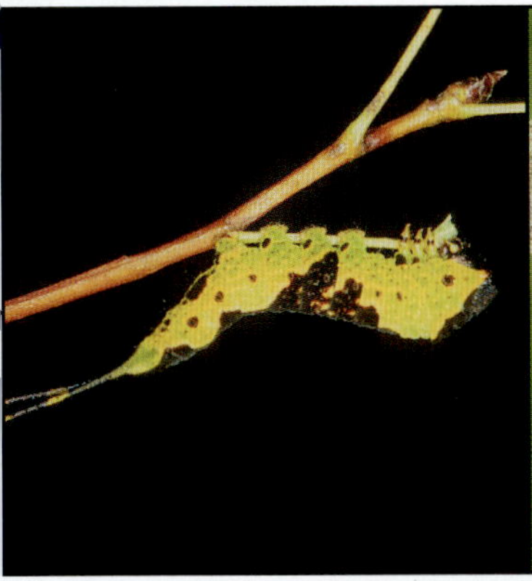

Western Furcula *Furcula occidentalis*

Modest Furcula *Furcula modesta*

Yellow-necked Caterpillar Moth *Datana ministra*

APRIL	MAY	JUNE	JULY	AUG	SEPT	OCT

Caterpillar Food: Many broadleaved woody plants

Nature Notes:

Caterpillars feed gregariously, in groups of tens to hundreds (inset photo) and often, when disturbed, arch and thrash about in a group display and may regurgitate gut contents.

Some populations seem recently reduced, perhaps further victims of a tachinid fly parasitoid introduced in a misguided effort at Spongy Moth (*Lymantria dispar*) control.

Moth: *Datana* adults are frustratingly similar, gray, tan, yellow-brown or brown, with darker red-brown over the thorax. *D. ministra* is large, and has a strongly scalloped outer forewing margin.

Caterpillar: Finely haired, black with yellow stripes and an orange prothoracic shield.

Life Cycle: One generation in our area. Pupa winters in soil or litter.

Range: Eastern U.S. and adjacent Canada; west to southern Manitoba. The similar Drexel's Datana (*Datana drexelii*) is rare in our region.

White-dotted Prominent *Nadata gibbosa*

APRIL	MAY	JUNE	JULY	AUG	SEPT	OCT

Caterpillar Food: Especially oaks, birches, alders and willows

Moth: Forewings yellow with rusty brown shading. Antemedial and postmedial lines thin but distinct. Reniform spot usually with a pair of silvery white dots. Females larger.

Caterpillar: Stout, waxy, blue-green, with a broken white subdorsal line. Spiracles orange. Head pale green, with black and yellow mandibles. Also yellow edging on anal plate.

Life Cycle: Perhaps a partial second generation in our area. Pupa winters underground.

Range: Across most of the U.S. and southern Canada; Newfoundland to British Columbia.

Nature Notes:

Adults are cryptic when perched on leaf litter with their heads pressed downward.

A dark (melanic) form has been reported.

The caterpillars bring to mind defended sawfly larvae (order Hymenoptera) in the way they curl up when disturbed and in the white dotting that suggests exuded toxic secretions.

Angulose Prominent *Peridea angulosa*

APRIL	MAY	JUNE	JULY	AUG	SEPT	OCT

Caterpillar Food: Mostly on oaks

Nature Notes:

An Angulose Prominent caterpillar I observed was an indefatigable eater that could not be bothered to have its determined meal interrupted. Despite repeated efforts to push it away with my finger, it kept right on at a very "business-like" clip.

Moth: Mottled gray forewings, with an irregular white patch in the median area near the costal margin and double black antemedial and postmedial lines filled with orange.

Caterpillar: Translucent green (sometimes pale red-brown), with yellowish spiracular stripe edged above with red, especially toward front.

Life Cycle: One generation. Pupa winters.

Range: Eastern U.S. and adjacent Canada; Nova Scotia to Manitoba.

Chocolate Prominent *Peridea ferruginea*

APRIL	MAY	JUNE	JULY	AUG	SEPT	OCT

Caterpillar Food: Mostly on birches

Moth: Mostly reddish-chocolate brown. White spot in the median area near the costal margin.

Caterpillar: Similar to Angulose Prominent but with spiracular stripe confined to head and thorax.

Life Cycle: One generation. Pupa winters.

Range: Northeast U.S. to Minnesota at northwest range limit; south in the Appalachians to Tennessee, North Carolina.

Nature Notes:

Five *Peridea* species occur in North America and at least two in Europe. Three species in our region.

Linden Prominent *Ellida caniplaga*

APRIL	MAY	JUNE	JULY	AUG	SEPT	OCT

Caterpillar Food: Basswood

Nature Notes:

Adults are cryptic, perching along stems with the narrow wings "cloaked" around them.

When caterpillars are disturbed they coil and show their shiny black mandibles.

Some caterpillars are quite plain, others gaudy. This could mean chemical defense varies strongly (odd, given one food plant species).

Moth: Forewings pale gray, mottled with brown and white. Antemedial line strong, dark, triple near costa. Reniform spot is a dark crescent surrounded by white.

Caterpillar: Pale green, striped with white and yellow and highly variably blotched with dark red on the dorsum. A large dark spot on each vertex of head makes identification easy.

Life Cycle: Apparently a partial second generation in our area. Pupa winters.

Range: Most of eastern U.S. and southern Canada; Minnesota is northwest range limit.

Mottled Prominent *Macrurocampa marthesia*

APRIL	MAY	JUNE	JULY	AUG	SEPT	OCT

Caterpillar Food: Mostly oaks; possibly also maples and poplars

Moth: Forewing dark at base, mottled white, gray and brown beyond antemedial line, which bends sharply at midpoint. Postmedial line double, filled with white. Black dash near anal angle. Often with green dashes.

Caterpillar: Pale green, with a red and yellow dorsal stripe, slanting yellow lateral stripes and a pair of straight, tapered stemapods (highly modified anal prolegs).

Life Cycle: One generation. Pupa winters.

Range: Widely in eastern North America and extending west to Arizona, Utah.

Nature Notes:

This is another species known to squirt acid at offending parties.

There are four known *Macrurocampa* species, both North American.

Oblique Heterocampa *Heterocampa obliqua*

APRIL	MAY	JUNE	**JULY**	AUG	SEPT	OCT

Caterpillar Food: Oaks

Nature Notes:

Like other prominent caterpillars, these have midventral defensive glands just behind the head. The degree to which they produce acid chemical deterrents is unclear.

Adults align with a twig, extend the hairy forelegs and with a rocking, side-to-side, settling-in motion, seem to mold themselves to the contours of the perch.

Moth: Forewing has a dark double antemedial line and a black, arching terminal dash. The large apical patch is conspicuous, whitish in males and pinkish brown in females.

Caterpillar: Pale green to reddish with a prominent white dorsal saddle. First three instars (third shown here) have conspicuous red antler-like projections on the first thoracic segment.

Life Cycle: One generation in our area.

Range: Through most of eastern U.S.; central Minnesota is northwest range limit. Mainly in southern part of our three-state region.

Double-lined Prominent *Lochmaeus bilineata*

APRIL	MAY	JUNE	JULY	AUG	SEPT	OCT

Caterpillar Food: Prefers elms and Basswood

Moth: Gray or gray-brown forewings; antemedial and postmedial lines double, sharper and less scalloped in *bilineata* than *manteo*.

Caterpillar: Highly variable in color and pattern. Sometimes with a broad, irregular, red saddle, bordered below with white and bisected by a continuous to broken white dorsal line; sometimes with little or no red. Paired raised warts on first and eighth abdominal segments.

Life Cycle: One generation. Prepupa winters.

Range: Common in most of eastern U.S.; mainly found in southern areas of our region.

Nature Notes:

The defensive spray of the closely related Variable Oakleaf Caterpillar Moth (*L. manteo*) can blister human skin, having formic acid contents of 20 to nearly 40 percent by volume. It has caused widespread defoliations of oak forests in Missouri and occurs north to central Ontario.

Chestnut Schizura *Schizura badia*

APRIL	MAY	JUNE	JULY	AUG	SEPT	OCT

Caterpillar Food: Viburnums

Nature Notes:

The caterpillars strongly resemble damaged leaves. The caterpillar blends well with blemishes on its food plants. It has a sloth-like disposition, moving very slowly.

Adults perch with their wings strongly tented.

Moth: Forewings gray, variably shaded with red-brown and a blackish reniform spot extended in a dark streak toward the outer margin.

Caterpillar: Mostly pale green with complex purple-brown shading on back, sides and head, and washed with bright yellow dorsally.

Life Cycle: Perhaps a partial second generation. Winter, perhaps variably, as pupae or prepupae.

Range: Through most of eastern U.S. and southern Canada; Nova Scotia to Manitoba.

Unicorn Caterpillar Moth *Coelodasys unicornis*

APRIL	MAY	JUNE	JULY	AUG	SEPT	OCT

Caterpillar Food: Many woody plants

Moth: Forewings complexly patterned in grays and browns with much yellowish shading along the costa and outside the postmedial line, with the veins darkly shaded. Basal area greenish.

Caterpillar: White **V** over abdominal segments six and seven. A large fleshy "horn" projects forward from the first abdominal segment and the eighth abdominal is strongly humped.

Life Cycle: One generation in our area. Prepupal caterpillars or pupae winter inside a cocoon.

Range: Most of eastern U.S. and all across northern tier of states and southern Canada; Newfoundland to northern British Columbia.

Nature Notes:

The caterpillars have midventral glands just behind the head, able to squirt formic and acetic acid several inches in a somewhat controlled direction. These glands can occupy a tenth of the caterpillar's volume. Some species also regurgitate possibly toxic gut contents.

Formerly *Schizura unicornis*.

Red-washed Prominent *Oedemasia semirufescens*

APRIL	MAY	JUNE	JULY	AUG	SEPT	OCT

Caterpillar Food: Especially on poplar and willow

Nature Notes:

Adults perch with their wings rolled into a tube and their heads pressed (often lowermost) against a branch, causing them to strongly resemble a twig stub (inset photo above).

There are four known species in North America and others further south. Three species in our area.

Moth: Streaked gray-brown forewings, washed with warm tones, especially along inner margin.

Caterpillar: Dorsum of the first abdominal segment projecting forward in a fleshy horn, complexly patterned in warm shades of brown, black and white.

Life Cycle: Perhaps a partial second generation in our area. Prepupa winters.

Range: Population concentrated in eastern U.S., Pacific Northwest and adjacent Canada; north to northern Alberta.

White-streaked Prominent *Ianassa lignicolor*

APRIL	MAY	JUNE	JULY	AUG	SEPT	OCT

Caterpillar Food: Favors oaks. Many broadleaved woody plants

Moth: Medium-sized, with streaked gray-brown forewings, washed with warm tones and contrastingly streaked.

Caterpillar: Dorsum of the first abdominal segment projecting forward in a fleshy horn, complexly patterned in brown, green and white.

Life Cycle: Perhaps a partial second generation in our area. Prepupa winters.

Range: Most of eastern U.S. and southern Canada; northwest range limit is southern Manitoba.

Nature Notes:

The caterpillars clearly outclass the adults in visual presentation. That is, once you actually see them. Casual observation will likely pass them over for just another tattered leaf.

Red-humped Oakworm Moth *Symmerista canicosta*

APRIL	MAY	JUNE	JULY	AUG	SEPT	OCT

Caterpillar Food: Oaks and possibly birch, elm, maple & basswood

Nature Notes:

The three *Symmerista* species in our region are often impossible to identify in the field. The other two are the more northerly Orange-humped Oakworm (*S. leucitys*) and White-headed Prominent (*S. albifrons*).

The caterpillar's bright rump patch which matches the head coloration may serve to confuse predators or deflect attack from the head to a less vital part.

Moth: Mottled gray forewings with inconspicuous black lines and an irregular white bar running along the costal margin from the antemedial line to the apex.

Caterpillar: Shiny, smooth black, yellow and white striped, with a shiny red-orange head and rump prominence. Five black stripes separated by four white stripes on its back

Life Cycle: One generation. Pupa winters.

Range: Sparsely across northeastern U.S.; south to South Carolina. Fairly uncommon in our three-state region.

Black-spotted Prominent *Dasylophia anguina*

APRIL	MAY	JUNE	JULY	AUG	SEPT	OCT

Caterpillar Food: Many legumes such as clovers and bush clovers

Moth: Dimorphic; females with yellow-brown forewings and dark hindwings; males pale gray, with pale hindwings; both streaked with black, with black and white lower postmedial lines and black spots in the lower subterminal area.

Caterpillar: Shiny smooth; blue, yellow, orange and black striped, with orange head and a shiny black bump on the eighth abdominal segment.

Life Cycle: One generation. Pupa winters.

Range: Eastern U.S. and southern Canada west to Colorado and Saskatchewan. Only very southern parts of our region.

Nature Notes:

Recorded June 25 to July 27 in western Ontario.

This is the only North American prominent that feeds on herbaceous plants instead of trees.

The caterpillar's gaudy coloration suggests chemical defense, but this seems untested.

Tiger & Lichen Moths
Family Erebidae
Subfamily Arctiinae

Moths of this subfamily are small to medium-sized, often colorful, moths perhaps best defined by the presence of sound-producing tymbal organs in adults and by laterally-paired dorsal pheromone glands in females. They have metathoracic tympanal hearing organs, directed rearward, each served by two sensory nerves. Many gather toxic chemicals from their larval food plants and/or as adults and advertise their defense by way of bright colors and bold patterns (aposematism) as well as by ultrasonic "back-talk" to bats. Moths with hearing and sound producing abilities fly more than those lacking them, perhaps improving their reproductive success.

Arctiids are remarkable for their use of defensive features (plant-derived defensive chemicals and ultrasonic signaling) in courtship. They are also remarkable for their widespread mimicry of wasps, best developed in the tropics, which has complicated interpretation of their phylogeny.

Moths
While the majority of North American species do not feed as adults, some do. This largely reflects the predominance of the large tribe Arctiini which shows a strong tendency toward mouthpart reduction. Many tropical arctiids feed as adults. There is a widespread tendency toward flightlessness in females (though not in our species). Some males have greatly reduced hindwings, but in their case flight is not impaired.

Caterpillars
Caterpillars mostly feed on herbaceous plants, others on lichens or mosses and some on trees and shrubs. They are typically densely hairy, with the setae arising from verrucae (wart-like elevations). Some (perhaps all) caterpillars are sensitive to low-frequency sound through setae. Hemispherical eggs usually laid in clusters.

Diversity (Species Richness/Range)
A 2016 North American checklist now includes 956 species in Erebidae of which nearly 300 species are in subfamily Arctiinae; about 50 of those found in our three-state region.

Little Shaded Lichen Moth *Clemensia umbrata*

APRIL	MAY	JUNE	**JULY**	**AUG**	SEPT	OCT

Caterpillar Food: Lichens, probably mostly for the algae within

Moth: Little white moth with forewings finely speckled with brown and black.

Caterpillar: Beaded, knobby, contrastingly marked with green, yellow, black and white, with sparse setae.

Life Cycle: One generation. Pupa winters.

Range: Across boreal Canada from Nova Scotia to Northwest Territories, British Columbia. New England south into the Appalachians and west to northern Great Lakes.

Nature Notes:

Recently split from *Clemensia albata* (Little White Lichen Moth) which is nearly identical but more eastern and southern and has a different flight phenology.

May feed at night, hiding during the day, though I found a caterpillar perched openly on a log in daylight. The coloration blends well with lichens.

Apparently feeding is constrained by dry spells.

Bicolored Moth *Manulea bicolor*

APRIL	MAY	JUNE	JULY	AUG	SEPT	OCT

Caterpillar Food: Lichens growing on conifers

Nature Notes:

Judging by their resemblance to toxic and distasteful lampyrid beetles (fireflies) these moths may be chemically defended, but this seems untested.

Many lichen moth caterpillars feed at night and hide during the day.

Lichen feeding may essentially be algae feeding, as many species do not seem to need associated fungal enzymes for digestion.

Moth: Forewing gray, yellow along costa. Pale yellow collar and tail tuft.

Caterpillar: Mottled brown and yellow-gray; black head and enlarged warts with clusters of short setae (based on a short description; no photo). To about 1.25 inches.

Life Cycle: Likely one generation in our area. Wintering stage undetermined.

Range: Only in Canada, Alaska and the very north of the U.S. from New England, New York west to the North Woods of our region, Montana, mountains of Wyoming, Colorado.

Scarlet-winged Lichen Moth *Hypoprepia miniata*

Black-and-yellow Lichen Moth *Lycomorpha pholus*

Painted Lichen Moth *Hypoprepia fucosa*

APRIL	MAY	JUNE	JULY	AUG	SEPT	OCT

Caterpillar Food: Lichens; likely primarily for the algae within

Moth: Forewings variably red, with three broad gray lines running along axis of wing. Body red, with gray on abdomen and thorax.

Caterpillar: Bristly, black and yellow, with black head and spines.

Life Cycle: One generation in our area. Caterpillar winters.

Range: Eastern U.S. and adjacent Canada west to edge of Rocky Mountains; Nova Scotia to Alberta and south to south Texas, Florida.

Nature Notes:

An apparent firefly (lampyrid beetle) mimic. Fireflies are often chemically defended by steroids and advertise this with patterns of red, yellow and black.

Adults are able to produce ultrasound.

Lichen-feeding moths can accumulate various compounds from lichens for defense.

Caterpillars sometimes cannibalistic.

Virgin Tiger Moth *Apantesis virgo*

APRIL	MAY	JUNE	JULY	AUG	SEPT	OCT

Caterpillar Food: Wide variety of herbaceous and woody vegetation

Nature Notes:

Apantesis caterpillars are often difficult to identify.

Patterns of *Apantesis* tiger moths are similar and variable enough to make identifications difficult. There are presently about 43 species in North America.

Formerly *Grammia virgo*.

Moth: The largest *Apantesis* species; forewing boldly black and white striped. Most easily told from similar species by black spots in the median area of the red hindwing.

Caterpillar: Black and stiffly bristled, with orangish spiracles and warts.

Life Cycle: One generation. *Apantesis* species winter as partly grown caterpillars, feeding and pupating in spring/early summer in thin silk cocoons containing larval hairs and concealed in leaf litter.

Range: Eastern U.S. and adjacent Canada; west to British Columbia.

Figured Tiger Moth
Apantesis figurata

Little Virgin Tiger Moth
Apantesis virguncula

Parthenice Tiger Moth *Apantesis parthenice*

APRIL	MAY	JUNE	JULY	AUG	SEPT	OCT

Caterpillar Food: Variety of herbaceous and woody vegetation

Moth: Quite similar to Virgin Tiger Moth, but smaller with finer lines and the hindwings lacking the lower two innermost black spots.

Caterpillar: Black and stiffly bristled; sometimes has some brown hairs and a pale dorsal line.

Life Cycle: One generation. Winter as partly grown caterpillars, feeding again and pupating in spring/early summer in thin silk cocoons containing larval hairs

Range: Most of the U.S.; west to Idaho, Utah, New Mexico. In Canada from Nova Scotia to British Columbia, Northwest Territories.

Nature Notes:

The caterpillars presumably are somewhat defended by the profusion of long hairs, but I am unaware of any test of their palatability to birds. Reportedly the British lepidopterist, H. B. D. Kettlewell, popped caterpillars into his mouth on occasion, as a quick and dirty way to assess their edibility to predators. It is perhaps best he didn't live in the tropics!

Formerly *Grammia parthenice*.

Harnessed Tiger Moth *Apantesis phalerata*

APRIL	MAY	JUNE	JULY	AUG	SEPT	OCT

Caterpillar Food: A variety of herbaceous plants

Nature Notes:

There are 43 North American *Apantesis* species of which 13 occur in our area.

Recent analysis of mitochondrial DNA yielded results that do not match well with current tiger moth species boundaries. There is evidence of broad genetic exchange between species, which ought not occur.

Adult *Apantesis* do not feed.

Moth: The mostly black forewing has a cream white costal edge and lines. The pattern varies, especially on the hindwing, which is more often yellow than red.

Caterpillar: Forbes describes the caterpillar as "dull black, usually with a pale dorsal line, hair brown of varying shades, sometimes nearly black."

Life Cycle: Likely two generations in our area. *Apantesis* pupae winters.

Range: Eastern U.S. south to Guatemala; only reaches southern parts of our region. Ruby Tiger is Holarctic; nearly to Arctic Ocean.

St. Lawrence Tiger Moth *Arctia parthenos*

APRIL	MAY	JUNE	JULY	AUG	SEPT	OCT

Caterpillar Food: Alder and willow Many broadleaved woody plants

Moth: Large, quite variable, with brown forewings marked with yellowish spots and bars. Orange-yellow hind wings are marked with heavy irregular dark lines.

Caterpillar: Similar to Great Tiger Moth caterpillar, but lacking reddish hair, and with brown spiracles and conspicuous pale lateral warts.

Life Cycle: One generation. Partly grown caterpillar winters.

Range: North Woods of our three-state region. New England to northern Alaska; Rocky Mountains; Canada nearly to Arctic Ocean.

Nature Notes:

Tiger moths have "ears" (basically bat detectors) tuned to the ultrasonic pulses used by hunting bats. They respond with organs known as tymbals which they vigorously flex, producing rapid series of ultrasonic pulses, to advertise their foul taste/toxicity, startle the bats or perhaps jam the bats' navigation system.

There are ten North American *Arctia* species; only two in our region.

Great Tiger Moth *Arctia caja*

APRIL	MAY	JUNE	JULY	AUG	SEPT	OCT

Caterpillar Food: Many broadleaved woody & herbaceous plants

Nature Notes:

Restricted to North Woods.

Adults can emit toxic yellow froth from dorsal thoracic glands while displaying bright hind wings and producing squeaking sounds audible to humans. Some defensive toxins are gathered by the caterpillars from their food plants, but those secreted by the adults may be synthesized "in-house."

Known as the "Garden Tiger" in England.

Moth: Forewings brown, with a bold network of white lines. Hindwings yellow-orange with four or five deep blue spots ringed in black.

Caterpillar: Dark haired, with red-orange hairs on front of thorax and low on abdomen. Skin black, spiracles white.

Life Cycle: One generation. Partly grown caterpillar winters.

Range: Restricted to colder climates. New England, New York to North Woods of our region; Rocky Mountains. Holarctic; England, mainland Europe, Scandinavia, Russia, Japan.

Virginian Tiger Moth *Spilosoma virginica*

APRIL	MAY	JUNE	JULY	AUG	SEPT	OCT

Caterpillar Food: Herbaceous and woody broadleaved plants

Moth: White with minute dark spots on wings. Yellow on abdomen and forelegs.

Caterpillar: Hairy, with considerable variation within and between species. Known as the "Yellow Bear."

Life Cycle: Partial second generation. Pupa winters in a cocoon that contains larval hairs.

Range: All across the U.S. and in Canada north to Northwest Territories. South to Florida, Texas, Mexico. Odd disjunct population around Beunos Aires, Argentina.

Nature Notes:

Three other similar white *Spilosomas* in our region: the Pink-legged Tiger Moth (*S. latipennis*) has pink forelegs and white body; Agreeable Tiger Moth (*S. congrua*) has yellow on the forelegs but not on the body; and the Dubious Tiger Moth (*S. dubia*) is similar to Virginian but with less yellow on its body. All but the Pink-legged have more-or-less minute dark spotting on the wings.

Giant Leopard Moth *Hypercompe scribonia*

APRIL	MAY	JUNE	JULY	AUG	SEPT	OCT

Caterpillar Food: Many broadleaved woody & herbaceous plants

Nature Notes:

Adults look warningly colored, but palatability to birds seems untested. They "bleed" yellow, acrid-smelling hemolymph from thoracic glands and display the colorful abdomen when disturbed.

Caterpillars can survive temperatures of 26.6 degrees F. with 45% of their body water frozen to ice, but perish when temperatures reach 14 degrees F. Glycerol is their antifreeze.

Moth: Forewing translucent white, with numerous hollow blue-black spots. Striking iridescent blue and orange markings on the large abdomen.

Caterpillar: Bristly black, with red intersegmental rings and yellow spiracles.

Life Cycle: One generation in our area. Partly grown caterpillar winters.

Range: Widely in eastern North America; more common in southern parts of our region, but now reaching into the North Woods of Minnesota; the most northerly North American locations.

Isabella Tiger Moth (Woolly Bear) *Pyrrharctia isabella*

APRIL	MAY	JUNE	JULY	AUG	SEPT	OCT

Caterpillar Food: A broad diet of herbaceous and woody plants

Moth: Forewings orange-brown, pointed, marked with brown lines and a dark reniform spot.

Caterpillar: Bristly, usually black at the ends, with a variable orange band between. When disturbed they drop, curl up head-to-tail and remain motionless. They can survive brief freezing, but do so better after prolonged acclimation than earlier in the fall.

Life Cycle: One generation in our area. Caterpillar winters.

Range: Most of U.S. and southern Canada; north to northern Alberta, south to Mexico.

Nature Notes:

Contrary to popular mythology, the caterpillars are no better than the National Weather Service at long-range winter forecasting.

Caterpillars are seen loping across trails and parking lots in the fall and spring. Why they move so much, when they can eat most anything, is a good question, though it could be to search for food rich in pyrrolizine alkaloids.

LeConte's Haploa *Haploa lecontei*

APRIL	MAY	JUNE	JULY	AUG	SEPT	OCT

Caterpillar Food: Especially plants in aster and borage families

Nature Notes:

Five of the six North American species are found in our region.

Adults perch conspicuously on low vegetation.

The bold skunk-like patterns and open perching suggest these moths are chemically defended and only a few of 24 adults were eaten by native birds in one study.

Adults produce ultrasound in response to bats.

Moth: Haploas are medium-sized, boldly-patterned, black and white moths often seen perched atop vegetation. All are similar and variable enough to make identification tricky.

Caterpillar: Variations of black and yellow stripes; black heads, many large dark warts studded with short, dark, stiff setae. *Haploa reversa* has a red dorsal stripe.

Life Cycle: One generation in our area. Partly grown caterpillar winters.

Range: All Haploas found widely in eastern U.S.; LeConte's is the most northerly species.

Other Haploa moths...

Confused Haploa *Haploa confusa*

The Neighbor *Haploa contigua*

Clymene Moth
Haploa clymene

Reversed Haploa
Haploa reversa

Banded Tussock Moth *Halysidota tessellaris*

APRIL	MAY	JUNE	JULY	AUG	SEPT	OCT

Caterpillar Food: Many broadleaved woody plants

Nature Notes:

Females gather pyrrolizidine alkaloids from decaying plant sources such as asters, joe-pye weeds and ragworts for purposes of defense and/or pheromone production. This is known as pharmacophagy.

The hairiness of the caterpillar likely provides defense against predators. Caterpillars eat their shed skins, hairs included, possibly to retain the defensive pyrrolizidine alkaloids.

Moth: Forewing pale yellow, with irregular pale brown bars outlined partly in black. Striking teal and yellow thorax stripes.

Caterpillar: Long-haired, yellow to gray, with long black and white hair "pencils" at front and rear.

Life Cycle: One generation in our area. Pupa winters.

Range: Mainly found in eastern U.S. and adjacent Canada. Some records in Rocky Mountains and south to Mexico.

Spotted Tussock Moth *Lophocampa maculata*

APRIL	MAY	JUNE	JULY	AUG	SEPT	OCT

Caterpillar Food: Especially poplar, willow, alder and hazel

Moth: Forewings deep yellow, with several irregular bands of pale brown.

Caterpillar: Hairy; dark on ends, with many long tufts of white hair; yellow in middle, with four black dorsal tufts.

Life Cycle: Likely one generation in our area. Pupa winters.

Range: Widely in U.S. and southern Canada; Newfoundland to Northwest Territories, Yukon. In our region found across Michigan, but mainly northern parts of Minnesota and Wisconsin.

Nature Notes:

The cocoon includes many larval hairs felted together with silk (inset photo below).

The conspicuous markings of caterpillars suggest chemical defense. And surely their hairiness affords some protection.

Caterpillars leave much evidence of their presence, such as ragged leaves. This suggests they do not fear birds.

Hickory Tussock Moth (*Lophocampa caryae*) is similar but caterpillar is white.

Delicate Cycnia Moth *Cycnia tenera*

APRIL	MAY	JUNE	JULY	AUG	SEPT	OCT

Caterpillar Food: Dogbanes

Nature Notes:

Also called Dogbane Tiger Moth.

Males produce clicks (mostly ultrasonic, but faintly audible to humans) in response to the ultrasonic pulses of hunting bats and in courtship. Males also release pheromones when near potential mates. Males deprived experimentally of both sound production and pheromones were shunned.

Moth: Forewing cream white with bright yellow on costa reaching nearly to apex. Head and abdomen yellow, abdomen with a series of black spots.

Caterpillar: With much fine, long, gray hair. Caterpillars gather and store toxic cardiac glycosides from dogbanes. Palatability to wild birds was rated low in one study.

Life Cycle: Likely a partial second generation in our area. Pupa winters.

Range: Widely in U.S. and southern Canada; Nova Scotia to British Columbia.

Milkweed Tussock Moth *Euchaetes egle*

APRIL	MAY	JUNE	JULY	AUG	SEPT	OCT

Caterpillar Food: Dogbanes and milkweeds

Moth: Wings and thorax unmarked, middle gray, with orange-yellow collar and abdomen, the latter with a series of black mid-dorsal spots.

Caterpillar: Dark, densely hairy, with numerous tufts of black, white and orange setae. Head shiny black.

Life Cycle: One generation in our area. Pupa winters.

Range: Most of eastern U.S. and southernmost Canada. Across our region but seems to be mostly absent from northeastern Minnesota.

Nature Notes:

Early-stage caterpillars feed in a close group that appears cryptic at a distance (like a patch of dead leaf). They chew through major leaf veins to disarm the pressurized copious latex of the food plants.

Adults produce ultrasonic clicks when approached by hunting bats, to warn, truthfully or not, of chemical defense.

Virginia Ctenucha *Ctenucha virginica*

APRIL	MAY	JUNE	JULY	AUG	SEPT	OCT

Caterpillar Food: Especially grasses, also sedges, irises

Nature Notes:

Commonly flies during day, feeding at flowers, but also comes to lights. Adults also gather pyrrolizidine alkaloids from various plant sources and males have abdominal coremata that release pheromones during mating.

Adults, with their iridescent blue hues, apparently mimic wasps.

Moth: Distinctive and frequently encountered. Forewings deep gray-brown, head and collar orange, body iridescent blue.

Caterpillar: Head red and black, prolegs red. Dorsal tufted hairs vary from white to black. Body dark, with broken, pale, subdorsal and subspiracular stripes.

Life Cycle: One generation. Caterpillar winters. Cocoons distinctive (inset below).

Range: Concentrated in northeastern U.S. (some southeast records) and southern Canada; Newfoundland to British Columbia.

Yellow-collared Scape Moth *Cisseps fulvicollis*

APRIL	MAY	JUNE	JULY	AUG	SEPT	OCT

Caterpillar Food: Grasses and sedges

Moth: Forewings long, narrow, blackish. Body blue-black, with an orange collar.

Caterpillar: Pale, sparsely tufted with hair from conspicuous warts, striped in several colors.

Life Cycle: Likely a partial second generation in our area. Caterpillar winters; how far north they can survive is unknown.

Range: Much of North America; Newfoundland to British Columbia and north to Northwest Territories. An annual immigrant to some parts of its northern range.

Nature Notes:

A wasp mimic, commonly seen perched on or feeding at goldenrod flowers during the day. Dead moths offered to native birds in one study were not eaten.

Apparently must re-colonize northern part of its range each year, being unable to survive winter.

Caterpillars are easily overlooked because they feed mostly at night and very close to the ground.

Tussock Moths
Family Erebidae
Subfamily Lymantriinae

Long-standing as a family, now widely viewed as a subfamily of Erebidae, itself split from the old inclusive Noctuidae largely on the basis of wing venation and nuclear DNA.

Moths

Adults cannot feed. Metathoracic tympanal ears are present and males may have sound-producing tymbal organs on the third abdominal segment. Females are usually larger than males and in some species have wings reduced to nubs or developed but not functional. Adults have a characteristic perching posture in which the forelegs are extended together in front. Eggs are often laid in large clumps and covered or mixed with irritating hair like scales and/or a frothy secretion.

Caterpillars

This family likely holds the record for duration of the caterpillar stage. The Arctic Woollybear (*Gynaephora groenlandica*) which feeds on dwarf tundra shrubs, takes nine to 14 years to pupate. The caterpillars feed alone, in North America on broadleaved and coniferous woody plants. Caterpillars often bear long tufts of hairs and irritant spines. Red or yellow button-like glands often occur in the dorsal midline on the sixth and seventh abdominal segments. The presumed defensive function of these glands seems little studied. The pupae are also hairy (as in many lasiocampids).

Diversity (Species Richness/Range)

Subfamily Lymantriinae: 32 species in North America, including about 12 in our area.

Other subfamilies within Family Erebidae

Subfamily Herminiinae (pages 176-177): Roughly 90 species in North America, including about 45 in our area.

Subfamily Hypeninae (pages 178-179): 32 species in North America, including about 16 in our area.

Subfamily Erebinae (pages 180-195): About 300 species in North America.

Spongy Moth (Gypsy Moth) *Lymantria dispar*

APRIL	MAY	JUNE	JULY	AUG	SEPT	OCT

Caterpillar Food: Over 500 broadleaved and coniferous woody plants

Moth: Highly dimorphic. Females large and whitish with dark spots and lines and large abdomens. Males much smaller, brown with yellow tones, thin abdomens; markings obscure.

Caterpillar: Final stage sparsely hairy, complexly marked in black and white, appearing dark gray. Conspicuous wart to either side of head.

Life Cycle: One generation. Mature caterpillars in May and June. Egg winters.

Range: Native to Europe and Asia. Introduced into Boston from France in 1869 and still extending its range.

Nature Notes:

Caterpillars cause allergic symptoms in many people either by touch or by windborne setae.

Most serious outbreaks occur in oak forests, possibly when low acorn production causes small mammal population declines, reducing their predation on caterpillars and pupae.

Well established in Michigan and Wisconsin, and moving into Minnesota (southeast, Twin Cities, North Shore).

Sharp-lined Tussock Moth *Dasychira dorsipennata*

APRIL	MAY	JUNE	JULY	AUG	SEPT	OCT

Caterpillar Food: Willows; many other broadleaved woody plants

Nature Notes:

The caterpillars sometimes cause allergic reactions, either when touched or through windborne setae.

Dasychira is exclusively North American, with 16 known species. (And yet there are 604 names—mostly junior synonyms—listed by one source! This likely reflects the difficulty of species-level identification.)

Moth: Like many other tussock moths, confusingly variable (inset photo) and difficult to identify to species. Rather than strain my powers of description, I offer photos of known reared adults.

Caterpillar: Fortunately, distinctive in having a single dark middorsal hair pencil (as well as two lateral ones) at the rear.

Life Cycle: One generation in our area. All *Dasychiras* winter as partly grown larvae.

Range: Much of northeastern U.S. south in mountains to North Carolina and west to Manitoba. Seven species in our region.

Streaked Tussock Moth *Dasychira obliquata*

APRIL	MAY	JUNE	JULY	AUG	SEPT	OCT

Caterpillar Food: Perhaps primarily oaks; broadleaved woody plants

Moth: Adult *Dasychiras* are exceptionally variable and difficult to identify. Typically perch with the forelegs extended out in front.

Caterpillar: Refreshingly distinctive for this genus, dull brown with stubby darker dorsal tufts and especially scant black caudal hair pencils.

Life Cycle: One generation in our area. Winter as partly grown caterpillars.

Range: Northeastern U.S. and southern Canada south to Georgia (in mountains); Minnesota is northwest range limit in North America.

Nature Notes:

The shed exuviae so much resemble the live caterpillars that I wonder if they serve some defensive purpose, perhaps by providing false and/or irritant targets to predators.

This is likely the most common *Dasychira* species in many areas.

Rusty Tussock Moth *Orgyia antiqua nova*

APRIL	MAY	JUNE	JULY	AUG	SEPT	OCT

Caterpillar Food: Many woody plants, preferring conifers

Nature Notes:

Males fly mostly during the day and rarely come to lights.

Searching for the handsome caterpillars on conifers in August and September may be the best way to find this species. Beating trays are helpful in searching conifers.

Pale eggs with black bull's-eyes winter in clusters on the outside of vacated female cocoons.

Moth: Male forewings rusty brown, with a pale crescent at the postmedial line near inner margin. Female has only tiny wing nubs.

Caterpillar: Dark gray, with broad black dorsal stripe, four conspicuous pale dorsal tufts and bright red warts.

Life Cycle: One generation in our area. Egg winters.

Range: Holarctic: Alaska, Northwest Territories to Newfoundland and across Europe, Russia, China. In U.S. more common from New England to Minnesota; also Pacific Coast.

Definite Tussock Moth *Orgyia definita*

APRIL	MAY	JUNE	JULY	AUG	SEPT	OCT

Caterpillar Food: Great many broadleaved and coniferous woody plants

Moth: Definite and White-marked Tussock Moths (*O. leucostigma*) are very similar and quite variable, making identifications difficult; the wingless females are nondescript. Since the caterpillars are distinctive, reared adults can be surely identified.

Caterpillar: Similar anatomy, but the yellow and pale gray of *definita* are mostly replaced by reds, blacks and whites in *leucostigma*.

Life Cycle: Two generations. Egg winters.

Range: Eastern U.S. and southern Canada. *O. leucostigma* more commonly reported.

Nature Notes:

Despite the gaudy caterpillar, that feeds messily in open daylight and is avoided by birds, the moths are readily eaten.

Flightless females lay eggs in large, froth-covered clusters on the outsides of their vacated cocoons.

Since females cannot fly to disperse eggs, most dispersal is achieved by early-stage caterpillars that drift on silk "balloons."

American Idia *Idia americalis*

APRIL	MAY	JUNE	JULY	AUG	SEPT	OCT

Caterpillar Food: Dead or living leaves and associated fungi

Nature Notes:

The ten species of *Idia* in our region, though easily overlooked, are important to forest nutrient cycling. Their caterpillars can be numerous, fragmenting and digesting leaf litter and even rotting wood, promoting its decomposition.

Non-native earthworms consume the leaf litter many native litter feeders (including these moths) depend on.

Moth: A large group of small moths, often drab and hard to identify. Many males have distinctive swellings of enlarged scales on their antennae. The labial palps are very long.

Caterpillar: Mostly drab brown and hard to tell apart; some have conspicuous dorsal knobs.

Life Cycle: Apparently multiple generations are common. Partly-grown caterpillars winter in the leaf litter.

Range: Widely in eastern U.S. and southern Canada; in our area many species reach only southern parts of our region.

Other Leaf Litter Moths...

Common Idia *Idia aemula*

Glossy Black Idia *Idia lubricalis*

Dark-banded Owlet *Phalaenophana pyramusalis*

Variable Zanclognatha *Zanclognatha laevigata*

Dark-spotted Palthis *Palthis angulalis*

Dimorphic Snout *Hypena bijugalis*

APRIL	MAY	JUNE	JULY	AUG	SEPT	OCT

Caterpillar Food: Dogwood. Most Hypena are specialized feeders

Nature Notes:

Adults are often flushed from the forest floor during the day.

Adults of this subfamily have laterally "lashed" compound eyes and very long, upturned labial palps, which have earned them the common name "snouts."

Most *Hypena* fly June through August, but some as early as May or as late as October.

Moth: Dimorphic Snout is sexually dimorphic. Most species cryptic, brown to black with long, upturned labial palps ("snout") and delta profile. In many species median area is contrastingly dark.

Caterpillar: Caterpillars are bright, translucent green and somewhat beaded. The first pair of prolegs is smaller and the hindmost prolegs are held splayed out behind.

Life Cycle: Mostly two generations. Pupa winters in a leaf-litter cocoon.

Range: Most occur widely in eastern North America.

Other Hypena Moths...

Green Cloverworm Moth *Hypena scabra*

Mottled Snout *Hypena palparia*

White-lined Snout *Hypena abalienalis*

Deceptive Snout *Hypena deceptalis*

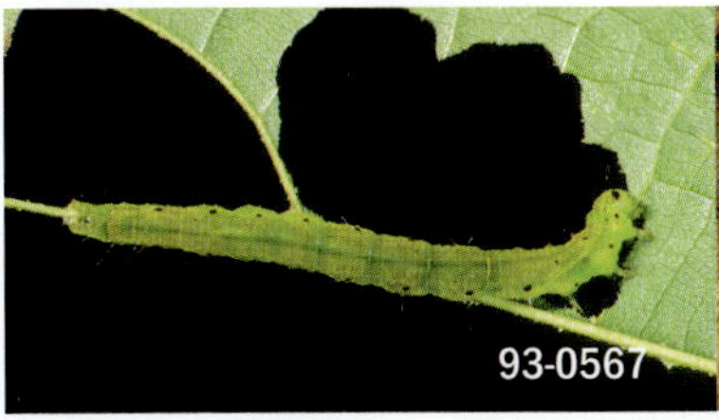

Large Snout *Hypena edictalis*

The Herald *Scoliopteryx libatrix*

APRIL	MAY	JUNE	JULY	AUG	SEPT	OCT

Caterpillar Food: Especially willows; also aspen, alder and birch

Nature Notes:

Among the longest lived adult moths, approaching a year. Feeding is necessary to such long life and they visit sugar baits.

Translucent caterpillars present a fine opportunity to observe the tracheal network branching out from the spiracles and other internal anatomy.

Wintering adults sometimes share quarters with hibernating bats.

Moth: Medium-sized, gray-brown, with bright orange patches and white postmedial lines and heavily scalloped forewing margins.

Caterpillar: Slender, translucent green, with yellow spiracular line.

Life Cycle: One generation. Mature caterpillars spin flimsy cocoons on their food plants and eclose within a couple of weeks. Adult winters in leaf litter, caves, hollow trees and logs, wells, foundations and other sheltered places.

Range: Holarctic; northern Quebec to Alaska and across Europe, Russia. Across the U.S.

Canadian Owlet *Calyptra canadensis*

APRIL	MAY	JUNE	JULY	AUG	SEPT	OCT

Caterpillar Food: Meadow-rues (*Thalictrum* species)

Moth: Forewing light brown with darker bands; postmedial line nearly straight, slanting from apex to inner margin. There are two scale tufts on the inner margin.

Caterpillar: Waxy white with black spots above. Sides bright yellow, lower body black. Head yellow with three black spots on each side.

Life Cycle: One generation in our area. Pupa winters.

Range: Most of eastern U.S. and southern Canada; Despite its common name, mostly found in the southern parts of our region.

Nature Notes:

Caterpillars resemble chemically defended sawfly larvae in their bright colors, bold markings, waxy luster and behavior of coiling and holding on, rather than dropping, when disturbed.

Relatives in Asia include male moths with powerful piercing probosci studded with tearing hooks, able to pierce fruit, or mammalian (including human) skin for blood.

Moonseed Moth *Plusiodonta compressipalpis*

APRIL	MAY	JUNE	JULY	AUG	SEPT	OCT

Caterpillar Food: Specialized on the vine Moonseed

Nature Notes:

Caterpillars strikingly resemble fresh bird droppings in color, shape and luster. By masquerading as bird droppings they avoid becoming them.

The vine Moonseed (*Menispermum canadensis*) occurs in Minnesota from the St Croix River valley to Red Lakes and south. This is one possible limit to the moth's distribution.

Moth: Forewing brown and metallic gold, with large scale-tuft projecting from hind margin.

Caterpillar: Distinctive pattern of dark brown, white, blue-gray and gold-brown, much resembling a bird-dropping. Only three pairs of prolegs. Perches with the anterior abdominal segments arched.

Life Cycle: Two generations in our area. Pupa winters.

Range: Most of eastern U.S. and southern edge of Canada; southern edge of our three-state region.

Common Fungus Moth *Metalectra discalis*

APRIL	MAY	JUNE	JULY	AUG	SEPT	OCT

Caterpillar Food: Various fleshy and woody fungi, especially on logs

Moth: Wings yellowish, heavily mottled with light to dark brown. Obscurely marked except for blackish reniform patches.

Caterpillar: Body strongly beaded (narrowed between segments), very rough, with enlarged, pale tubercles, missing prolegs on third and fourth abdominal segments; mottled brown with dark subdorsal bar-like patches.

Life Cycle: Probably one generation. Pupa winters in cocoon of silk and excavated rotted wood.

Range: Most of eastern U.S.; Minnesota to Nova Scotia and south to Brazil, Bolivia.

Nature Notes:

Caterpillars are usually only occasionally found, but can be, at least locally and briefly, abundant. Search moist rotten logs on the forest floor, especially at night.

Many caterpillars that feed on fungus, or on dead plant material associated with fungus, appear to rely partly on fungal enzymes for digestion.

Six-spotted Gray *Spargaloma sexpunctata*

APRIL	MAY	JUNE	JULY	AUG	SEPT	OCT

Caterpillar Food: Dogbanes

Nature Notes:

Dogbanes contain cardiac glycosides, known for their effect on vertebrate heart muscle and sometimes stored by caterpillars (and sometimes retained into adults) for chemical defense. Given the cryptic appearance of these caterpillars and adults, they likely don't do so, but their palatability to birds is apparently unstudied.

Moth: Forewings purplish-gray with a dark median band sharply edged basally and fading gradually distally.

Caterpillar: Translucent, smooth, green, unmarked, somewhat beaded (narrower between segments).

Life Cycle: The long flight period suggests (but does not prove) two generations. Pupa winters.

Range: Across northern U.S.; in Canada from Nova Scotia to British Columbia.

Thin-lined Owlet *Isogona tenuis*

APRIL	MAY	JUNE	JULY	AUG	SEPT	OCT

Caterpillar Food: Hackberry

Moth: Forewings brownish gray, the lines, veins and margin of the reniform spot yellowish white, the antemedial and postmedial lines most prominent.

Caterpillar: Slender, gray, with numerous dark and light warts with dark hairs and many fine stripes. Head speckled.

Life Cycle: Two generations likely. Pupa winters in a rolled-leaf-edge cocoon.

Range: A more southerly species that just reaches the southern portions of our three-state region.

Nature Notes:

The northwestern range limits of this species (and many others) have long been under-reported, but as of 2025 the most northerly record on iNaturalist is central Minnesota.

Once-married Underwing *Catocala unijuga*

APRIL	MAY	JUNE	JULY	AUG	SEPT	OCT

Caterpillar Food: Once-married on poplars and willows

Nature Notes:

Nearly 60 species of *Catocala* species in our region. Most fly from mid-summer into September.

Adults perch head-down on tree trunks where forewing patterns blend with bark. When disturbed they launch explosively, flashing the strongly patterned and colorful hindwings as they fly rapidly and erratically to suddenly disappear again. Hindwings may serve to startle or as targets, deflecting attack away from head and body.

Moth: Medium-sized to large, forewings cryptic, with bark-like patterns and hindwings often boldly patterned and/or brightly colored.

Caterpillar: Twig-like, cryptically marked in gray, brown and black, often with conspicuous knobs, warts and fringes of setae along ventral.

Life Cycle: One generation. Eggs winter in bark crevices or leaf litter for eight months, hatching near bud break in spring. Pupate in thin cocoons in leaf litter.

Range: About 30 species reach only southern areas of our region; about five to central Ontario; and five more to northern Ontario.

Other Underwings...

White Underwing *Catocala relicta*

Pink Underwing *Catocala concumbens*

Ultronia Underwing *Catocala ultronia*

Praeclara Underwing *Catocala praeclara*

Similar Underwing *Catocala similis*

Clover Looper *Caenurgina crassiuscula*

APRIL	MAY	JUNE	JULY	AUG	SEPT	OCT

Caterpillar Food: Especially herbaceous legumes

Nature Notes:

These very common moths are active day and night. They are often flushed when walking through herbaceous ground cover or seen feeding at flowers at dusk.

Also known as "The Double-barred."

Similar Forage Looper (*C. erechtea*) has forewing bands that do not reach inner margin. Flies into November.

Moth: Gray forewings crossed by dark bands that converge near the inner margin, almost meeting near the inner margin and touch it. Males are better marked; females are larger.

Caterpillar: Slender, tapered, tan to pinkish, with many wavy stripes and first two pairs of prolegs absent (leaving three). Broad pale stripe below spiracles. Stripes extend onto the head.

Life Cycle: Multiple generations. Pupa winters.

Range: Through much of U.S. and southern Canada, north to central Alaska. Figure-seven Moth only in southern Lower Michigan.

Toothed Somberwing *Euclidia cuspidea*

APRIL	MAY	JUNE	JULY	AUG	SEPT	OCT

Caterpillar Food: Many herbaceous plants; clovers, grasses, lupines

Moth: Forewing purplish to yellowish brown, with strong deep brown antemedial band, basal and apical marks and postmedial line triangle.

Caterpillar: Many longitudinal tan to brown stripes that continue onto the head. Belly dark. Prolegs on the fourth abdominal segment are undersized. Similar to Forage and Clover Loopers, which lack prolegs on the fourth abdominal segment.

Life Cycle: Likely one generation. Pupa winters.

Range: Eastern U.S. and southern Canada west to Washington and British Columbia.

Nature Notes:

These moths fly day and night and come readily to light.

The pattern of perched adults resembles a Rorschach inkblot test. Many see faces.

There are five known species in North America and others in the Old World.

Short-lined Chocolate *Argyrostrotis anilis*

APRIL	MAY	JUNE	JULY	AUG	SEPT	OCT

Caterpillar Food: Likely wild plums and other cherries; possibly roses

Nature Notes:

Apparently very uncommon in our area. I have seen only one (at light) on June 17 in east central Minnesota.

The bold markings of this elegant moth might signal chemical defense but apparently this has not been tested. Alternatively, perhaps they serve to make the true outline harder for predators to see, thus being disruptive.

Moth: Forewings chocolate brown, crossed by sharp white antemedial and partial postmedial lines.

Caterpillar: Pale violet, with pink stripes and brown raised ridges across fifth and eighth abdominal segments.

Life Cycle: One generation in our area. Pupa winters.

Range: Widely in eastern U.S.; few and widely scattered records from across our region.

Black Witch *Ascalapha odorata*

Huge moth (6 inch wingspan) that is literally blown into our region from the southern U.S. during hurricane events. Males lack white band.

Maple Looper *Parallelia bistriaris*

APRIL	MAY	JUNE	JULY	AUG	SEPT	OCT

Caterpillar Food: Especially red & other maples, also birches & walnuts

Moth: Forewings deep brown, with straight thin yellowish antemedial line and similar but gently wavy postmedial line and pale dusting beyond subterminal line.

Caterpillar: Shades of gray, brown or red, with a distinctive black line running foreward on each side of head. Eighth abdominal segment with a black-edged ridge.

Life Cycle: Possibly two generations in our area. Pupa winters.

Range: Eastern U.S. and southern Canada, onto southern Great Plains.

Nature Notes:

Though sometimes flushed from the forest floor during the day, these moths also come to lights and sugar baits.

These moths are well hidden on leaf litter, especially on fallen maple leaves, their heads pressed down. Yet, in a feeding test, dead moths were rated only "moderately acceptable" to wild birds, so apparently they also have some chemical protection.

Horrid Zale *Zale horrida*

APRIL	MAY	JUNE	JULY	AUG	SEPT	OCT

Caterpillar Food: Viburnums; perhaps especially Nannyberry

Nature Notes:

Striking in their ability to disappear on tree bark. The patterned hindwings reflect their usual partial exposure in the characteristic perching posture. The One-lined Zale (*Zale unilineata*) (opposite page) more likely perches on leaf litter.

Maple Zale (*Z. galbanata*) (opposite page) with two protracted generations, flys into September.

Moth: Very distinctive, with a strongly undulating subterminal line that divides the black inner portion from a strongly contrasting outer whitish band.

Caterpillar: Finely mottled in grays and browns. Have all five pairs of prolegs, but the front two pairs are reduced in size. Like those of underwing moths, twiglike and muscular, but lack a ventral fringe of setae.

Life Cycle: One generation. Pupa winters.

Range: About 14 wide-ranging species occur in the three-state region.

Other Zales...

Lunate Zale *Zale lunata*

Maple Zale *Zale galbanata*

Colorful Zale *Zale minerea*

Brown-spotted Zale *Zale helata*

One-lined Zale *Zale unilineata*

Locust Underwing *Euparthenos nubilis*

APRIL	MAY	JUNE	JULY	AUG	SEPT	OCT

Caterpillar Food: Black Locust, a southern tree, now naturalized here

Nature Notes:

The bright hindwings do not indicate chemical defense, since ten dead adults were readily eaten by wild birds, but may be a bluff, draw bird attacks away from the head and body, or simply startling birds, giving the moths a split-second head start at escape.

The caterpillars are robust, leaping and thrashing about powerfully, when disturbed.

Moth: Forewings gray-brown, with darker lines and a bold white slash beyond postmedial line at costa. Hindwings orange, with four bold wavy black lines.

Caterpillar: Stout, warm brown, with pinkish brown head freckled with white and reddish spiracles ringed in black. Sometimes with a distinctive subdorsal crescent of four white spots on first abdominal segment.

Life Cycle: Two generations. Pupa winters.

Range: Much of eastern U.S. and southern Canada; southern part of our region.

Red-lined Panopoda *Panopoda rufimargo*

APRIL	MAY	JUNE	JULY	AUG	SEPT	OCT

Caterpillar Food: Oaks and Blue Beech

Moth: Forewings yellow-brown with antemedial and postmedial lines mostly straight, thin, yellow and red or brown. Pale yellowish reniform spot sometimes strongly filled with black.

Caterpillar: Pale green, with white subdorsal stripe and pale lines running down and back over abdominal segments; finely pale-and-dark speckled.

Life Cycle: One generation in our area. Pupa winters.

Range: Much of eastern U.S.; More common in Wisconsin and Michigan in our region.

Nature Notes:

Adults generally cryptic and readily eaten by native birds in one study.

There are four known *Panopoda* species, all North American.

Dark Marathyssa *Marathyssa inficita*

APRIL	MAY	JUNE	JULY	AUG	SEPT	OCT

Caterpillar Food: Sumac and Poison Ivy

Nature Notes:

Adults have a striking perching posture in which forewings are held out, folded like pleated fans and the abdomen arched strongly upward so they resemble broken twig stubs or curls of bark.

The Light Marathyssa (*M. basalis*) occurs in the southern edge of our region. Its forewings are paler, with more yellow shading. They fly in May.

Moth: Forewing gray and chocolate brown, with red shading toward apex. Markings less distinctive than perching posture.

Caterpillar: Pale green, translucent, widest at thorax. White subdorsal stripe, body sparsely speckled with white, hairless, smooth. Spiracles orange. Turns crimson as a prepupa.

Life Cycle: Reportedly, at least two generations throughout its range. Pupa winters.

Range: Eastern U.S. and southern Canada, north and west to Manitoba; scattered sightings across our region.

Eyed Paectes *Paectes oculatrix*

APRIL	MAY	JUNE	JULY	AUG	SEPT	OCT

Caterpillar Food: Poison Ivy

Moth: The curved arc of the postmedial line creates a dramatic pattern in the outer forewing that, in the perching posture, strongly suggests vertebrate eyes.

Caterpillar: Translucent pale green, unmarked, somewhat beaded (constricted between segments).

Life Cycle: Likely one brood in our area. Pupa winters.

Range: Much of eastern U.S. and southern Canada, west to Manitoba; only scattered records in our region.

Nature Notes:

Whether the bold eye-like markings of adults intimidate predators, obscure the body outline or warn of chemical defense is unknown, but two dead moths offered to birds were not eaten.

Rarely have I seen this moth at lights, even amidst dense populations.

Caterpillars are well hidden under poison ivy leaves into which they chew ragged holes.

Tuft Moths Family Nolidae

Until recently these moths were placed in two or three subfamilies of Noctuidae and before that in Arctiidae. The tuft moths now have their own family.

Moths

They are small to medium-sized and have metathoracic tympanal hearing organs. Some have patches of raised scales on the forewing cells. The wings are coupled by a frenulum and retinaculum and the latter is bar-shaped.

Caterpillars

The caterpillars of Nolidae have conspicuous clusters of setae on raised warts and lack prolegs on the third abdominal segment. Those of Risobinae are green with prominent subdorsal stripes, short prolegs and very few setae.

Diversity (Species Richness/Range)

There are about 1700 described species worldwide and they are most diverse in the Old-World tropics. The 39 North American species are placed in seven subfamilies, with about 15 species in our region. All members construct boat-shaped cocoons with a slit-like exit valve.

Eyed Baileya *Baileya opthalmica*

Doubleday's Baileya *Baileya doubledayi*

APRIL	MAY	JUNE	JULY	AUG	SEPT	OCT

Caterpillar Food: Alders

Moth: Forewing boldly marked, gray with a slightly curved, oblique, white postmedial line and a black "teardrop" reniform spot.

Caterpillar: Bright translucent yellow-green, with a strong yellow subdorsal and irregular-edged white addorsal line.

Life Cycle: Possibly two generations. Pupa winters inside a spindle-shaped cocoon of chewed fragments bound together with silk along a twig or leaf midvein.

Range: Much of eastern U.S. and southern edge of Canada; Nova Scotia to Saskatchewan.

Nature Notes:

Four other *Baileya* species in our region, most are smaller, drabber and more southerly.

Note unique adult perching posture (inset photo).

The cocoons, with a vertical exit-valve slit at one end, were recently recognized as a feature uniting the family Nolidae.

Some *Baileya* caterpillars are shiny enough to resemble sawfly larvae.

Owlet Moths
Family Noctuidae

The taxonomy of the superfamily Noctuoidea (which includes/or included Arctiidae, Notodontidae, Lymantriidae, Pantheidae, Nolidae, and Noctuidae and likely more than 75,000 species, world-wide) has long been confused, is in rapid flux, and will likely remain so for decades to come. Presently the old inclusive Noctuidae is widely split (largely on the basis of wing venation and nuclear DNA studies) into a more restricted Noctuidae and a segregated family Erebidae in which the old Arctiidae and Lymantriidae are included as subfamilies. At lower taxonomic levels (e.g. species and genus), DNA barcoding, which compares sections of mitochondrial DNA, is discovering (in conjunction with other studies) a large number of previously overlooked, superficially similar species and providing often surprising insights into the relationships between species.

Moths

Adults are stout, very small to large and often drab. Most have developed mouthparts and presumably feed as adults. There is a metathoracic tympanal hearing organ and a midventral prothoracic gland. The wings are coupled by a frenulum and retinaculum.

Caterpillars

Owlet caterpillars are widely diverse in size, shape, hairiness, "wartiness," color, markings, diet and behavior. In some groups such as dagger moths and Cucullias the caterpillars are remarkably more diverse than the adults. In other groups, such as the Agaristines, adults are more diverse than the caterpillars. Most have a full set of five pairs of prolegs, but some, known as loopers or semi-loopers for their modified gait, have the front one or two pairs reduced in size or absent. While many caterpillars feed on green plant tissues, many others feed on dead leaves, fungi, lichens, or even other caterpillars. Some, known as cutworms, variously climb vegetation to feed, feed at the surface of the soil, or burrow beneath the surface.

Diversity (Species Richness/Range)

A 2016 source names 2522 North American species in Noctuidae.

Spectacled Nettle Moth *Abrostola urentis*

APRIL	MAY	JUNE	JULY	AUG	SEPT	OCT

Caterpillar Food: Stinging Nettle and perhaps other nettles

Moth: Forewing gray, complexly mottled and shaded with brown, basal area not strongly contrasting.

Caterpillar: Complexly patterned in green and olive green, abdomen obliquely striped with double dark-over-light bands.

Life Cycle: Likely two generations in our area. A tiny caterpillar found on Stinging Nettle in east central Minnesota on July 1 yielded an adult on July 26. Pupa winters.

Range: Northeastern U.S. to Pacific Northwest; Nova Scotia to British Columbia.

Nature Notes:

I find caterpillars often in east central Minnesota, only on Stinging Nettle (*Urtica dioica*) and never on Wood Nettle (*Laportea canadensis*).

Caterpillars blend well visually with nettles and might even gain some protection by close association with stiff plant hairs loaded with irritating chemicals.

Hologram Moth *Diachrysia balluca*

APRIL	MAY	JUNE	JULY	AUG	SEPT	OCT

Caterpillar Food: Wood Nettle; also hops, aspen and raspberry

Nature Notes:

A splendid, much overlooked, somewhat uncommon, golden-green beauty. May be the largest plusiine in the world.

This dazzling moth markedly shifts brightness and color—gold, black, brown, purple and green—with angle of view—resulting from the way light interacts with the microstructure of the scales.

My records from Minnesota mostly from July.

A.k.a. Green-patched Looper.

Moth: Splendid, unmistakable, metallic gold-green. The coloration is largely structural and shifts appearance with changing angle of view.

Caterpillar: Pale green and white, with many large wart-like bumps and long sparse hairs. Only three pairs of prolegs.

Life Cycle: Partial second generation. Middle-instar caterpillar winters. I have seen grown caterpillars in the second half of May and one on September 15.

Range: Northeastern U.S. and southern Canada; Nova Scotia, Quebec to Alberta.

Straight-lined Looper *Pseudeva purpurigera*

APRIL	MAY	JUNE	JULY	AUG	SEPT	OCT

Caterpillar Food: Early and Tall Meadow-rue

Moth: Forewing light rusty brown, with indistinct gold-yellow areas. Postmedial line is gently curved, then sharply angled near the costa.

Caterpillar: Variegated green and white, with first through fourth and eighth abdominal segments greatly enlarged dorsally and bearing conical tubercles, those on the second and third abdominal segments distinctly tipped with black.

Life Cycle: One generation in our area. Middle-instar caterpillar winters.

Range: Northeastern U.S. and south in the Rocky Mountains to Colorado; Newfoundland to British Columbia.

Nature Notes:

The caterpillar much resembles that of the Pink-patched Looper (next page), but is easily distinguished by the dark spots at the apex of the conical projections on the first and second abdominal segments. The complex green and white markings allow both to blend very well with the intricate foliage and pale flowers of meadow-rues.

Pink-patched Looper *Eosphoropteryx thyatyroides*

APRIL	MAY	JUNE	JULY	AUG	SEPT	OCT

Caterpillar Food: Meadow-rues and Wild Columbine

Nature Notes:

Eosphoropteryx translates, poetically, as "dawn bearing wing," doubtless in reference to the forewing colors.

The plusiines have compound eyes heavily "lashed" laterally.

This sole member of its genus is generally uncommon.

Moth: Forewing narrow, with a pink base and pink shading beyond the postmedial line and along the costa; otherwise shaded dark gray, with white stigmatal spots. There is a distinct dorsal scale tuft on the third abdominal segment.

Caterpillar: Similar to that of Straight-lined Looper, but without distinct black subdorsal warts on second and third abdominal segments.

Life Cycle: One generation. Middle-instar caterpillar winters.

Range: Across northern U.S., especially in Northeast and Northwest and southern Canada; our area to northern Ontario.

Spruce False Looper *Syngrapha viridisigma*

APRIL	MAY	JUNE	JULY	AUG	SEPT	OCT

Caterpillar Food: Especially conifers; also blueberries & poplars.

Moth: *Syngrapha* species widely varied as a group. Forewings often mottled patterns of gray, black, white or brown, often with a darker medial area and a silvery white or greenish stigmatal mark. Hindwings often yellow-brown or yellow-orange with a dark border.

Caterpillar: Green with a dark dorsal stripe and other stripes strongly white.

Life Cycle: One generation. Middle-instar caterpillar winters.

Range: Spruce False Looper: northern tier of states, Rocky Mountains; north to central Alaska.

Nature Notes:

A holarctic genus of 32 species, 24 in North America, mostly associated with boreal and montane coniferous forests.

Caterpillar diet breadth apparently varies widely, some apparently feeding on many woody species.

A dozen *Syngrapha* species in our three-state region.

White-streaked Looper *Plusia venusta*

APRIL	MAY	JUNE	JULY	AUG	SEPT	OCT

Caterpillar Food: Grasses; possibly also sedges and bur-reeds

Nature Notes:

White-streaked is associated with wetlands and apparently uncommon.

Adults perch head-down along grass stems where the bold white streak may blend with highlights.

Putnam's is known as "Lempke's Gold-spot" in Europe.

Connected Looper more common south of the boreal forest in our region.

Moth: Forewing costa pinkish tan, remainder brown with a sharp white streak and pale inner and outer margins. Connected Looper has longer single (joined) silver stigma. Putnam's stigma consists of two separate silver marks.

Caterpillar: Slender, translucent green, with strong pale yellow spiracular line and thin yellowish dorsal and subdorsal lines.

Life Cycle: One generation in our area. Middle-instar caterpillar winters.

Range: New England to northern Alberta; mostly northern part of our area.

Other Plusiine Loopers...

Putnam's Looper
Plusia putnami

Connected Looper
Plusia contexta

Common Looper
Autographa precationis

Bilobed Looper
Megalographa biloba

Celery Looper
Anagrapha falcifera

Alfalfa Looper
Autographa californica

Large Mossy Protodeltote *Protodeltote muscosula*

APRIL	MAY	JUNE	JULY	AUG	SEPT	OCT

Caterpillar Food: Grasses

Nature Notes:

Eggs were laid (in captivity) in long rows inside the tightly rolled whorls of grass leaves. Many grasses were rejected and an unidentified delicate forest understory species was favored.

Grasses and sedges are sometimes infected with endophytic fungi that produce alkaloids that make the plants toxic to herbivores, including caterpillars.

Also known as Large Mossy Glyph.

Moth: Forewing heavily shaded with olive-brown and streaked with black; lower outer area commonly white.

Caterpillar: Slender, pale tan or green, with contrastingly dark dorsal line flanked by white addorsal and subdorsal lines; dark subspiracular line heaviest on thorax and lateral hind proleg. Proleg absent on third abdominal segment and much reduced on fourth.

Life Cycle: One generation. Pupa winters.

Range: Most of eastern U.S. and southern edge of Canada west to Manitoba.

The Brother *Raphia frater*

APRIL	MAY	JUNE	JULY	AUG	SEPT	OCT

Caterpillar Food: Aspens and willows

Moth: Forewing gray, postmedial line flattened near middle of curve. Hindwing white, with a dark patch at the anal angle.

Caterpillar: Translucent green, with many yellow dots; a strong transverse yellow crescent crosses first, fifth and eighth abdominal segments. Second thoracic segment with conical red dorsal projections.

Life Cycle: Two generations. Pupa winters in a cell chewed into rotted wood.

Range: Widespread across U.S. and southern Canada; Nova Scotia to British Columbia.

Nature Notes:

The significance of the common name eludes me; perhaps a reference to the drab, "monk-like" appearance?

The former Abrupt Brother (*R. abrupta*) is now considered the same species based on a lack of difference in mitochondrial DNA.

Olive-shaded Bird-dropping Moth

Ponometia candefacta

APRIL	MAY	JUNE	JULY	AUG	SEPT	OCT

Caterpillar Food: Ragweeds

Nature Notes:

Olive-shaded is known to be in Europe, likely as an introduction.

The Prairie Bird-dropping Moth (*P. binocula*) occurs in remnant prairies and may reach the southern part of our area. Very similar to *candefacta*, but without olive shading.

Moth: Forewing is white basally and along the costa and olive-shaded in the median and subterminal area. A dark gray arc, widest at the inner margin, reaches the apex. Head is white.

Caterpillar: Slender, green, humped at rear, with three pairs of prolegs. Head pattern lacking black is diagnostic.

Life Cycle: One generation. Pupa winters.

Range: Broadly in the eastern U.S.; more common in southern portions of our three-state region.

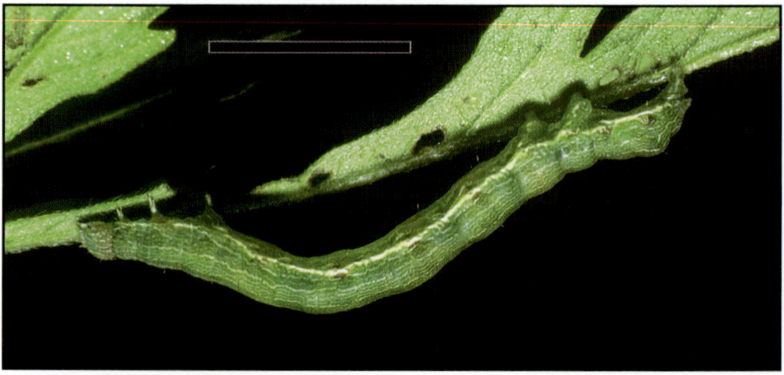

Small Bird-dropping Moth *Ponometia erastrioides*

APRIL	MAY	JUNE	JULY	AUG	SEPT	OCT

Caterpillar Food: Ragweeds

Moth: Like the Olive-shaded Bird-dropping Moth but without the olive shading. Its dark gray patch does not reach the apex. Its head is dark.

Caterpillar: Brown, tan, or green. Humped at rear, with three pairs of prolegs. White cheek patch divided by a black line is diagnostic.

Life Cycle: One generation. Pupa winters.

Range: Through the U.S.; more common in southern portions of our three-state region.

Nature Notes:

These little moths masquerade as bird droppings to avoid becoming them.

There are 29 North American *Ponometia* species and others in tropical and temperate South America. Five in our region.

Owl-eyed Bird-dropping Moth *Cerma cora*

APRIL	MAY	JUNE	JULY	AUG	SEPT	OCT

Caterpillar Food: Cherries; especially Pin Cherry

Nature Notes:

I reared two of these caterpillars found on Pin Cherry (*Prunus pensylvanica*) on July 8 in east central Minnesota. I've only seen one adult at lights. Apparently this is a truly rare moth, but rarity is harder to ascertain than commonness.

This beautiful moth resembles a patch of lichen when perched.

Also known as The Agate.

Moth: Except for white basal and median areas, forewings are mostly deep sage green, with many double, broken, irregular, black lines. A white reniform spot with a dark inner ring accounts for the common name.

Caterpillar: Broad, irregular, yellow, orange and white lateral band and broken white dorsal line. Many raised black warts bearing dark hairs.

Life Cycle: One generation in our area. Pupa winters in a cell chewed into rotted wood.

Range: Eastern U.S. and southern Canada; reaches northwest range limit in Minnesota.

Tufted Bird-dropping Moth *Cerma cerintha*

APRIL	MAY	JUNE	JULY	AUG	SEPT	OCT

Caterpillar Food: Esp. cherries, but also apple, juneberries, hawthorns

Moth: Forewings a complex pattern of black and white, with shadings of blue-gray, red-brown and olive green. Reniform spot white, with olive shading. Dark scale tufts on abdomen.

Caterpillar: Dark reddish above the white subdorsal stripe and green below it, with long dark hairs. Head shiny green with black stripes.

Life Cycle: One generation in our area. Mature caterpillars in July and August. Pupa winters inside a cell chewed into rotted wood.

Range: Eastern two-thirds of the U.S. and southern Canada to Manitoba.

Nature Notes:

I once brought a specimen home from the lighted side of a building only to find myself fooled by a bird dropping!

Eastern Panthea *Panthea furcilla*

APRIL	MAY	JUNE	JULY	AUG	SEPT	OCT

Caterpillar Food: Many conifers, including Tamarack, pines & spruces

Nature Notes:

Adults apparently are unable to feed.

Larvae referred to as Tufted White Pine Caterpillars.

Found in mixed and coniferous forests.

Subfamily Pantheinae was once considered a full family, Pantheidae. There are 16 North American species.

Moth: Forewings gray, crossed by several heavy, dark, wavy lines.

Caterpillar: Dark gray, with a complex pattern of white, black and orange variegations; sparsely long-haired, with long tufts of black hairs on first and eighth abdominal segments and orange setal warts. Often has irregular white patches near the white spiracles of the first eight abdominal segments.

Life Cycle: One generation. Pupa winters.

Range: Much of eastern U.S.; Canada from Nova Scotia, northern Quebec to Alberta.

Black Zigzag *Panthea acronyctoides*

APRIL	MAY	JUNE	JULY	AUG	SEPT	OCT

Caterpillar Food: Balsam Fir, Tamarack, Eastern Hemlock, pines, spruces

Moth: Boldly marked with black and white. Black orbicular spot surrounded by white. Checkered fringe.

Caterpillar: Distinctive; called Tufted Spruce Caterpillar. Black with white spots and whitish tufts of hairs, some long.

Life Cycle: One generation. Pupa overwinters in soil or debris.

Range: Quite northern in range; most common from New England across southern Ontario and Quebec to the North Woods of our three-state region.

Nature Notes:

Also called Tufted Spruce Caterpillar.

Seven species of *Panthea* in North America north of Mexico; two in our region.

Close-banded Yellowhorn *Colocasia propinquilinea*

APRIL	MAY	JUNE	JULY	AUG	SEPT	OCT

Caterpillar Food: Many broadleaved woody plants

Nature Notes:

"Yellowhorn" refers to the orange antennae.

A dark (melanic) form is known.

Adults appear unable to feed.

The Yellowhorn (*C. flavicornis*) is very similar. It is found in the very northern parts of our three-state region and northwest to northern Ontario, Manitoba, Saskatchewan.

Moth: Obscurely marked, grayish moth with orange antennae. Black lines are more or less vague, with the medial area darker near the inner margin.

Caterpillar: Variably white to black, with many bristly white setae, also a pair of black or rust-colored tufts on the thorax and unpaired mid-dorsal orange tufts on first and eighth abdominal segments. Head black or orange.

Life Cycle: One generation. Pupa winters.

Range: Widely in eastern North America; more records in Wisconsin and Michigan.

The Laugher *Charadra deridens*

APRIL	MAY	JUNE	JULY	AUG	SEPT	OCT

Caterpillar Food: Many broadleaved woody plants

Moth: Forewings mottled gray, complexly marked with broken, wavy, black lines. Orbicular spot white, with a central black dot.

Caterpillar: Variably pale to dark greenish-gray, with many long pale secondary setae; head shiny black with bright yellow markings on front.

Life Cycle: Two generations. Pupa winters.

Range: Widespread and common across eastern U.S. and southern Canada; our area to northern Ontario and Manitoba.

Nature Notes:

The common name likely refers to markings that suggest a laughing face in pinned specimen position.

Adults have functional mouthparts and presumably feed.

Unusually dark (melanic) and pale forms are known.

Three species of *Charadra* in North America; only this one in our area.

The Asteroid *Cucullia asteroides*

APRIL	MAY	JUNE	JULY	AUG	SEPT	OCT

Caterpillar Food: Aster family; Often prefer flowers but will eat leaves

Nature Notes:

Adults resemble broken off twigs in their perching posture, wings cloaked and their thoracic "hoods" raised.

In Europe they are commonly called "sharks" in reference to the prominent "fins" of thoracic setae formed when the patagia of the collar are raised.

Moth: Forewings narrow and pointed, pale gray to brown, variously streaked. Identifications of *Cucullia* species is difficult, involving subtleties of coloration in the fore- and hindwings or (surest) internal reproductive anatomy.

Caterpillar: Stout, smooth, boldly striped in green, yellow and white. Also a purplish form.

Life Cycle: One generation. Pupa winters underground.

Range: Ranges widely in North America; more common in southern portions of our three-state region.

Brown-hooded Owlet *Cucullia convexipennis*

APRIL	MAY	JUNE	JULY	AUG	SEPT	OCT

Caterpillar Food: Aster family; Often prefer flowers but will eat leaves

Moth: Distinct from other *Cucullias* in its warm brown tones. Forewings narrow, pointed and streaked.

Caterpillar: Stout, smooth and boldly striped in red, blue, black, yellow and white.

Life Cycle: One generation. Pupa winters underground.

Range: Ranges widely in North America; northwest range limit in the U.S. is north central Minnesota.

Nature Notes:

The bold, bright caterpillars suggest chemical defense, though some such as *asteroides* may be cryptic on their food plants, even in their purplish form (goldenrods often have some purplish leaves and stems).

Adults commonly feed at flowers at dusk.

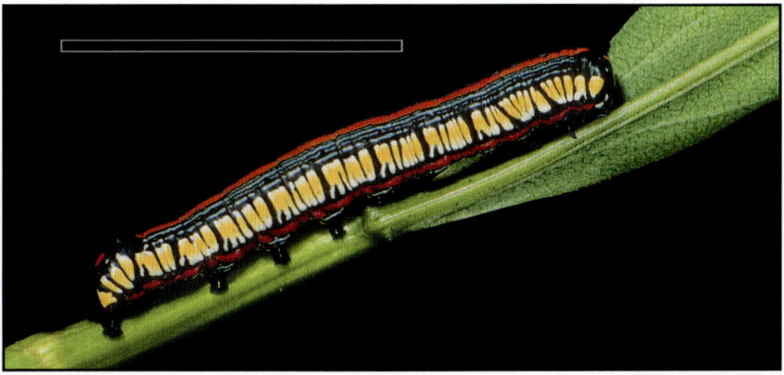

Harris's Three-spot *Harrisimemna trisignata*

APRIL	MAY	JUNE	JULY	AUG	SEPT	OCT

Caterpillar Food: Viburnums and other woody plants

Nature Notes:

When disturbed it rocks rapidly side to side. It carries around a series of its own shed head capsules, presumably for camouflage.

In color, texture and pattern, the caterpillar strongly resembles a dried bird dropping.

Pupation occurs in a cell chewed into rotted wood.

Moth: Forewings white, with irregular, broken, black lines and three large dull red spots. Hindwings white in males, gray in females. Often perches vertical (inset photo).

Caterpillar: Shiny, black and white, eighth abdominal segment hugely humped. Third through eighth abdominal segments saddled with white that streaks down the prolegs.

Life Cycle: One generation in our area. Pupa winters.

Range: Much of eastern North America; west to Texas, South Dakota, central Alberta.

Green Marvel *Acronicta fallax*

APRIL	MAY	JUNE	JULY	AUG	SEPT	OCT

Caterpillar Food: Viburnums

Moth: Pale green forewings with large irregular black spots overall. Hindwings white, faintly marked.

Caterpillar: Rich, translucent green, very cryptic inside the notch it has eaten into the leaf edge starting at the base.

Life Cycle: A (partial?) second generation is possible in our area. Pupa winters.

Range: Eastern U.S. west to eastern Minnesota, Oklahoma, east Texas; southern Canada from Newfoundland to Alberta.

Nature Notes:

Could be confused with the Green Leuconycta (*Leuconycta diphteroides*) on page 231, which has dark markings only at the costa of the forewing and gray hindwings.

Eight dead adults offered to birds were all eaten, indicating little if any chemical defense.

Splendid Dagger Moth *Acronicta superans*

APRIL	MAY	JUNE	JULY	AUG	SEPT	OCT

Caterpillar Food: Mostly rose family: cherries, juneberries, hawthorns

Nature Notes:

Why the caterpillars differ so much more than the adults is an intriguing question (see opposite page).

The common name "dagger moth" refers to the black dashes on the forewings of most species. Wingspans range from 1 to 2.5 inches.

A mostly holarctic genus with 79 North American species.

Moth: One of our larger and more distinctive dagger moths, with pale gray forewings, strong, diffuse basal and anal dashes that blend with dark shading in the median area, and conspicuous yellow shading in the basal area.

Caterpillar: Often more distinctive than the adults. Medium-sized, more or less hairy and often strikingly colored. Mostly 1.25 to 2 inches.

Life Cycle: Perhaps two generations here. Pupa winters in a cell chewed into rotted wood.

Range: In our area about 15 species occur only in our south and another 30 or so reach central and even northern Ontario.

Other Dagger Moth caterpillars...

American Dagger
Acronicta americana

93-1421

Miller Dagger
Acronicta vulpina

93-1427

Cherry Dagger
Acronicta hasta

93-1441.2

Eclipsed Oak Dagger
Acronicta increta

93-1419.87

Ochre Dagger
Acronicta morula

93-1444.3

Smeared Dagger
Acronicta oblinita

93-1485

Large Gray Dagger
Acronicta insita

93-1423

Powdered Dagger
Acronicta impleta

93-1474

Interrupted Dagger
Acronicta interrupta

93-1441.3

Cottonwood Dagger
Acronicta lepusculina

93-1425

Marsh Dagger *Acronicta insularis*

APRIL	MAY	JUNE	JULY	AUG	SEPT	OCT

Caterpillar Food: Cattails, grasses, sedges, smartweeds, aspen & willow

Nature Notes:

The caterpillars sometimes cause considerable damage to cattails in Florida.

I have at times seen many caterpillars on Reed Canary Grass in east central Minnesota. My caterpillar dates range June 23 through October 4, with many in September.

Formerly *Simyra insularis*.

A.k.a. Henry's Marsh Moth.

Moth: Forewings narrow, pale tan, with three brown streaks running toward outer margin.

Caterpillar: Complexly patterned in white and black, with several rows of bright orange warts bearing tufts of setae; dorsum mostly black.

Life Cycle: Likely two generations in our area. Pupa winters.

Range: Much of U.S. and southern Canada; our area to northern Ontario; more common in southern parts of our three-state region.

Beautiful Wood-nymph *Eudryas grata*

APRIL	MAY	JUNE	JULY	AUG	SEPT	OCT

Caterpillar Food: In our area primarily grapes, hops and woodbine

Moth: Forewings and body boldly patterned in white and dark brown, with complex shadings of yellow-green and blue-gray. The hindwings mostly yellow, with partial brown borders.

Caterpillar: Boldly ringed in black, white and orange, with black dots in orange bands and on darker orange head; thoracic shield orange. Rear strongly humped.

Life Cycle: One brood in our area. Pupa winters in a cell chewed into soft wood.

Range: Much of eastern U.S. and southern Canada; northern Michigan across to central Minnesota.

Nature Notes:

The Pearly Wood-nymph (*E. unio*) has a scalloped border between the white forewing and paler, redder outer margin (see inset photo). Caterpillar feeds on Fireweed and evening primroses.

Complex olive and white shadings strongly suggest a fresh bird dropping, complete with highlights, the splayed white legs even suggesting splash marks!

Grapevine Epimenis Moth *Psychomorpha epimenis*

APRIL	MAY	JUNE	JULY	AUG	SEPT	OCT

Caterpillar Food: Grape foliage, feeding inside folded-leaf shelters

Nature Notes:

Adults feed at flowers of apples, cherries and plums.

Presumably the bright colors and bold markings of caterpillars and adults advertise chemical defense, especially at close quarters. At greater distance or in low, greenish, forest light, the same colors might conceal.

Moth: A pretty little day-flier of early spring. Forewings black with large white patches, hindwings mostly red.

Caterpillar: Dull white, with many black and white rings; head, prothorax and hind abdominal segments orange with black spots.

Life Cycle: One generation. Caterpillars mature in late spring. Pupa winters.

Range: Much of eastern U.S.; north to central Michigan across to central Minnesota.

Eight-spotted Forester *Alypia octomaculata*

APRIL	MAY	JUNE	JULY	AUG	SEPT	OCT

Caterpillar Food: Grapes and woodbine

Moth: A dark little day-flying moth with two large pale yellow spots on each forewing and two large white spots on each hind wing. Also yellow on shoulders (tegulae) and bright orange on first two pairs of legs.

Caterpillar: Attractively ringed in black, white and orange. Sparse, long white hairs.

Life Cycle: One generation in our area. Pupa winters in a cell chewed into rotted wood.

Range: Most of U.S. and south edge of Canada west to Rocky Mountains; mostly southern parts of our three-state region.

Nature Notes:

Two similar species in our region: Langton's Forester (*Alypia langtoni*) with smaller forewing spots in males, flying in early June in northern Wisconsin. Also compare to White-spotted Sable on page 275.

Adults feed at flowers, including Fireweed and Common Milkweed.

Many-dotted Appleworm Moth *Balsa malana*

APRIL	MAY	JUNE	JULY	AUG	SEPT	OCT

Caterpillar Food: Foliage of the rose family: apple, cherry, plum

Nature Notes:

White-blotched Balsa (*Balsa labecula*) evidently the most northerly (and most common). It has a pale greenish patch in the upper median area.

Whether the caterpillars are cryptic or aposematic is a good question, but the adults are surely cryptic.

The Appleworm Moth has been introduced to eastern Asia where it is a pest.

Moth: Gray, more or less streaked forewings with lines near the costa and the postmedial split. Paler near the costa, lines thin and black.

Caterpillar: Stout, translucent green with numerous pale yellow dots. I have only seen two (both grown, on apple) in east central Minnesota

Life Cycle: One or possibly two generations in our area. Pupa winters.

Range: Eastern U.S. and southern Canada; few records in our three-state region.

Common Pinkband *Ogdoconta cinereola*

APRIL	MAY	JUNE	JULY	AUG	SEPT	OCT

Caterpillar Food: Ragweed, beans, sunflowers

Moth: Forewings dark brown, with a broad pink band along outside of the postmedial line. Other lines pale, thin, inconspicuous.

Caterpillar: Slender, green, with white dorsal, subdorsal, spiracular and subventral lines. Head with two white stripes on each side.

Life Cycle: Likely two generations in our area. Pupa winters.

Range: Much of eastern U.S.; perhaps only to southern portion of our region.

Nature Notes:

Except for the white stripes, this green caterpillar is quite translucent, offering an especially good look at the tracheal network radiating internally from the spiracles. The heart beat is clearly visible in the dorsal area as pulses flowing forward in rapid rhythm.

Green Leuconycta *Leuconycta diphteroides*

APRIL	MAY	JUNE	JULY	AUG	SEPT	OCT

Caterpillar Food: Goldenrods and asters

Nature Notes:

There are two known *Leuconycta* species, both North American.

Also called Green Owlet.

Moth: Forewing pale green (yellowish white in older specimens). Lines double, composed of small white dots. Black collar and two angular black patches along costa. Hindwing gray with darker border.

Caterpillar: Smooth, slender and green; striped with white dorsal and subdorsal lines and a pink spiracular line at ends of body.

Life Cycle: One generation in our area. Pupa winters.

Range: Most of eastern U.S. and barely reaching into southern Canada in our area.

Marbled-green Leuconycta *Leuconycta lepidula*

APRIL	MAY	JUNE	JULY	AUG	SEPT	OCT

Caterpillar Food: Dock and Common Dandelion

Moth: Quite variable. Adults are gray-green with large green orbicular and reniform spots lined with white and a darker brown to black median area, especially along the costa.

Caterpillar: Green with a yellowish head, prothoracic and anal plate. Some with broad red lateral stripes and some with broad white stripes edged above with darker green.

Life Cycle: One generation in our area. Pupa winters.

Range: More common in southern portions of our three-state region.

Nature Notes:

More southerly than Green Leuconycta.

The caterpillar variation noted in the description, occurred within one brood of reared eggs.

Copper Underwing *Amphipyra pyramidoides*

APRIL	MAY	JUNE	JULY	AUG	SEPT	OCT

Caterpillar Food: A wide variety of broadleaved woody plants

Nature Notes:

Adults gather in dark nooks and crannies, perhaps brought together by aggregation pheromones. This sometimes draws the disapproval of homeowners–"hideous" is one adjective I've heard.

The copper-red hindwings may startle, warn, bluff or deflect predators when they are flashed at take-off.

Moth: Forewings shades of gray, with an irregular postmedial line usually accented with white. Hindwings coppery red (usually only briefly visible at launch)(inset photo above).

Caterpillar: Chunky, blue green, with strongly humped rear, many yellow spots and a strong yellow spiracular stripe. Spiracles black with white rims.

Life Cycle: One generation. Egg winters.

Range: Across the continent; north to central Saskatchewan and Alberta.

Comstock's Sallow *Feralia comstocki*

APRIL	MAY	JUNE	JULY	AUG	SEPT	OCT

Caterpillar Food: Fir, spruce, Hemlock, possibly other conifers

Moth: Forewings bright green, fading to yellowish. Three large squared black blotches surround the reniform spot.

Caterpillar: Dark green with strong, broken white stripes, the spiracular one edged above with red.

Life Cycle: One generation. Mature caterpillars in early summer. Pupa winters.

Range: West across Canada south to Pacific Northwest and northern forests of Minnesota, Wisconsin and Michigan.

Nature Notes:

Well-suited to hide on lichened conifer trunks.

The deep green caterpillars with strong white lines blend in well among conifer needles.

Six species known from northern and mountain regions of North America; also one in Japan and eastern Russia.

Two other more or less green species in our area, early spring through early summer.

The Joker *Feralia jocosa*

APRIL	MAY	JUNE	JULY	AUG	SEPT	OCT

Caterpillar Food: Balsam Fir, Eastern Hemlock, spruces, pines

Nature Notes:

An early season moth in the northern states, often appearing in early April.

Moth: Bright green moth of spring. Reniform spot surrounded mainly by green (compare with Comstock's Sallow on page 233).

Caterpillar: Resembles that of Comstock's Sallow. A green caterpillar with white stripes is perfectly camouflaged when feeding on needles.

Life Cycle: Before the onset of winter, adults develop inside the pupa. They are now prepared to emerge early in the spring.

Range: Nova Scotia to British Columbia; New England south in Appalachians to Georgia; Idaho, Montana, Washington.

Fringe-tree Sallow *Sympistis chionanthi*

APRIL	MAY	JUNE	JULY	AUG	SEPT	OCT

Caterpillar Food: Leaves of ash trees

Moth: Forewing shades of gray with antemedial and postmedial lines and outlines of spots sharp black. Orbicular and reniform spots pale, with darker centers.

Caterpillar: Gray-brown with a wide dorsal line expanded into diamond-shapes over the thorax and anterior abdominal segments and a strong black subdorsal line from first through seventh abdominal segments. Humped at rear.

Life Cycle: One generation. Egg winters.

Range: Northeastern U.S. to our region; southern Canada; Quebec to eastern Alberta.

Nature Notes:

Caterpillars bear strong resemblance to the twigs and buds of ash, where they perch head down along twigs.

If the imported Asian Emerald Ash Borer beetle continues its onslaught (having already killed around 30 million ash trees of all species and age classes in Michigan) this is another dietary specialist that could face decline.

Purple-lined Sallow *Pyrrhia exprimens*

APRIL	MAY	JUNE	JULY	AUG	SEPT	OCT

Caterpillar Food: Wide range of woody and herbaceous plants

Nature Notes:

The Bordered Sallow (*P. cilisca*) is quite similar but with more orange in the forewings and lacks the sharply-bent median line. The hindwing is yellowish with a reddish margin. It flies mid June through early August and reaches central Ontario.

Caterpillars often favor flowers and fruits into which they bore.

Moth: Forewing dull orange, markings and shadings dark brown, with little reddish caste. Note sharply bent median line. Hindwing yellowish with a broad dark brown border.

Caterpillar: Variably colored, shiny, with scattered dark warts bearing setae. More or less black and white dorsal striping, black true legs and on prolegs. A broad orange spiracular stripe.

Life Cycle: One generation in our area. Pupa winters in soil.

Range: Holarctic, including much of eastern U.S. and southern Canada to northern Ontario.

Primrose Moth *Schinia florida*

APRIL	MAY	JUNE	JULY	AUG	SEPT	OCT

Caterpillar Food: Flowers, fruits, seeds of evening primroses (*Oenothera* spp)

Moth: A bright moth with forewings mostly deep pink to the wavy postmedial line and bright yellow beyond. Hindwings unmarked.

Caterpillar: Mostly green, with a darker mid-dorsal stripe and variable pink shading, especially on the thorax and anterior supraspiracular area. Sparsely covered with short white setae.

Life Cycle: One generation. Pupa winters.

Range: Across the U.S.; southern Canada from Newfoundland to British Columbia.

Nature Notes:

Flight period coincides with the blooming of its host plants—several species of evening primroses.

The caterpillars much resemble the green developing fruits of evening primroses.

Somewhat uncommon, adults are sometimes found during the day perched inside the partly closed flowers of evening primroses (inset photo).

Boreal Gem *Heliothis borealis*

Rarely encountered day-flying moth of open bogs in the boreal forest. Fast flight. May to June. Maroon wingtips. Quebec to Alberta. Only U.S. records: Northern Minnesota, Wisconsin, U.P. of Michigan.

Ragweed Flower Moth *Schinia rivulosa*

APRIL	MAY	JUNE	JULY	AUG	SEPT	OCT

Caterpillar Food: Ragweeds

Nature Notes:

A mostly North American genus of 121 known species (about 40 in the eastern half), comprising the bulk of the subfamily Heliothinae here. There are a few in the Old World.

Some *Schinia* species are day-flying; they have smaller eyes than night-fliers.

Moth: Forewings powdery gray-brown, darker brown in basal area and beyond the postmedial line. The smoothly convexly curved antemedial and broadly zig-zag postmedial lines are boldly marked with white.

Caterpillar: Dark gray above and below a broad pale green and white spiracular/subspiracular band. Spiracles orange ringed with black.

Life Cycle: One generation. Pupa winters.

Range: Most of eastern U.S.; southern part of our three-state region.

Arcigera Flower Moth *Schinia arcigera*

APRIL	MAY	JUNE	JULY	AUG	SEPT	OCT

Caterpillar Food: Specialists, mostly on asters

Moth: Male forewings warm purple-brown, females grayer brown, both with contrastingly darker basal area. Antemedial line roundly convex, postmedial line smoothly and broadly sinuous, both contrastingly marked with white.

Caterpillar: Chunky, pale brown above a contrasting white subspiracular line. Spiracles black, rimmed with white. Thoracic shield is black.

Life Cycle: One generation. Pupa winters.

Range: Through most of eastern U.S.; occurs mainly in southern part of our area, with scattered records to northern Minnesota.

Nature Notes:

Schinia caterpillars feed especially on flowers, fruits and seeds, the earliest stages concealed within. In at least some species (e.g. *S. lucens*, on Leadplant) pupation is well underground, perhaps as a way to survive prairie fires.

Pink-shaded Fern Moth *Callopistria mollissima*

APRIL	MAY	JUNE	JULY	AUG	SEPT	OCT

Caterpillar Food: Ferns. Silver-spotted on Sensitive & Bracken Ferns

Nature Notes:

Caterpillars rest on ferns during the day, where they visually match the broken pattern of green shadows and light.

Both red and green form caterpillars can appear in the same brood.

My only wild-caught caterpillar was from Lady Fern in early August in east central Minnesota.

Silver-spotted (upper inset) much less common than Pink-shaded.

Moth: Forewing warm reddish brown, with many broken dark brown lines and areas of pink shading. Reniform spot has a silver outline. Silver-spotted red-brown with distinctive large white (silver) spots on forewings.

Caterpillar: Green or reddish, with oblique white patches above abdominal spiracles. Each side of head with two dark vertical lines.

Life Cycle: Apparently at least a partial second generation in our area. Pupa winters.

Range: Eastern U.S. and southern Canada. Reaches northwest range limit in Minnesota.

Pink-barred Pseudeustrotia *Pseudeustrotia carneola*

APRIL	MAY	JUNE	JULY	AUG	SEPT	OCT

Caterpillar Food: Docks, smartweeds and goldenrods

Moth: Forewing mostly dark brown to the postmedial line and tan beyond it. A wide pink band crosses the dark area from the costa toward anal angle.

Caterpillar: Olive-brown or pale green, with a broad pale spiracular stripe that runs down the side of the hind proleg.

Life Cycle: Either one protracted generation and two generations. Pupa winters.

Range: Most of eastern two-thirds of U.S. to Montana, Colorado; Canada from Newfoundland to western Alberta.

Nature Notes:

This moth might be a bird-dropping "mimic;" others are so elaborate there is little doubt. Presumably such high-level disguises develop through more basic stages. Perhaps this is one such. Or perhaps a rough resemblance is sometimes good enough.

There is just one North American species and a number throughout the Old World.

Spotted Phosphila *Phosphila miselioides*

APRIL	MAY	JUNE	JULY	AUG	SEPT	OCT

Caterpillar Food: Several greenbrier species

Nature Notes:

Caterpillars perch and feed on the undersides of greenbrier leaves. When disturbed they curl back on themselves and pull their heads into the thorax, but do not drop from the plant.

How this species uses and tracks the distribution of, the five species of greenbriers (*Smilax*) that enter our area in Minnesota, is unknown.

Moth: Forewings olive green to brown, indistinctly mottled and marked, except for a distinct white reniform spot, which is obscured in darker individuals.

Caterpillar: Chunky, pale translucent green, with bright yellow dots. Smooth, with very inconspicuous setae. Head pale tan. Turns black (except for yellow spots) as a prepupa.

Life Cycle: One extended generation (or two?) in our area. Pupa winters.

Range: Eastern U.S. and southern Canada; southern edge of our three-state region.

Immigrant Pinion *Lithophane oriunda*

MARCH	APRIL	MAY	JULY	AUG	SEPT	OCT

Caterpillar Food: Cherries (Adults feed on sap, flowers of maple, willow)

Moth: Forewings red-brown with the costal area contrastingly white. The orbicular and reniform spots are pale or have pale inner rings and the former is elliptical.

Caterpillar: Dark with conspicuous diagonal markings; dorsum shaded with orange. The cervical shield is black. Broad, dark spiracular line and a wide pale subspiracular line.

Life Cycle: One generation. Adult winters.

Range: Apparently only southeastern Canada and northern tier of eastern states. Reported as local and uncommon by Forbes.

Nature Notes:

Adults do not mate until late winter or early spring. Some may fly almost any winter night when temperatures rise above freezing. Such long adult life requires feeding at sap flows or early flowers of maples or willows. Since these chunky moths are heavily wing-loaded, they must warm their flight muscles by shivering to fly at low temperatures.

Formerly known as Oriunda Pinion.

The Wedgling *Galgula partita*

APRIL	MAY	JUNE	JULY	AUG	SEPT	OCT

Caterpillar Food: Wood-sorrel species

Nature Notes:

An annual migrant from the south, likely unable to survive winter in our area.

With many hundreds of species in the host plant family (Oxalidaceae), records of caterpillars feeding on them are remarkably few, perhaps owing to high concentrations of oxalic acids (also high in rhubarb leaves), known to kill sheep on occasion.

Moth: Dimorphic: male forewings red-brown to pale gray; female dark maroon-brown. Both have a large dark spot on the costa and angled white-edged dark antemedial and postmedial lines.

Caterpillar: Much swollen first abdominal segment and less so at eighth, with white dorsal and thin subdorsal lines; a white lateral line, touching the tops of most spiracles.

Life Cycle: Migrant to our region but does not breed here.

Range: Most of U.S. south to Central America and West Indies; our area to northern Ontario.

Pale-winged Midget *Elaphria alapallida*

APRIL	MAY	JUNE	JULY	AUG	SEPT	OCT

Caterpillar Food: Box Elder; also dead leaves

Moth: Forewing brown, with a distinct white reniform spot embedded in a broad black dash.

Caterpillar: Dark brown, strongly humped at rear, with a red dorsal line and white subdorsal lines on thoracic shield.

Life Cycle: Likely one generation in our area. Pupa winters, in a shallow chamber chewed into bark and roofed over with the silk-bound tailings.

Range: Eastern U.S. to edge of Rocky Mountains; Nova Scotia, Quebec to British Columbia.

Nature Notes:

Two or three other midget species occur in our area, all in our south.

Reported larval diets are widely diverse. Either they are specialists or their diets are so poorly known that they only seem different. Some may feed on dead plant tissues.

These little moths are easily overlooked and other species likely await discovery.

Cloaked Marvel *Chytonix palliatricula*

APRIL	MAY	JUNE	JULY	AUG	SEPT	OCT

Caterpillar Food: Fruiting bodies of fungi growing on wood

Nature Notes:

Many caterpillars that feed on dead leaves or rotted wood may also need associated fungi to digest their food. Caterpillars that live in fungus-rich habitats such as leaf litter show a variety of traits such as complexly sculpted body surfaces, long setae, filters over the spiracular openings and use of silk tunnels to minimize contact with potentially pathogenic fungi and prevent wetting.

Moth: Obscurely marked with blackish basal and median areas and only a short white dash in the lower median area (main photo); or forewings pale brown with large white patches in median area (photo below).

Caterpillar: Plump brown, with a small pale head crossed side-to-side by two black "horizontal" lines; whitish setal warts.

Life Cycle: Likely one generation in our area. Pupa winters.

Range: Much of northern half of U.S. and southern Canada; our area to central Ontario.

Gray Half-spot *Nedra ramosula*

APRIL	MAY	JUNE	JULY	AUG	SEPT	OCT

Caterpillar Food: Several species of St. Johnswort

Moth: Forewing boldly streaked with black, white, gray and brown; lower half of reniform spot outlined in white.

Caterpillar: Shades of warm brown with a strong pale yellow subspiracular line that runs from antennae to tip of hind prolegs. Chunky at rear tapered forward to small head.

Life Cycle: Likely two generations in our area. Pupa winters.

Range: Much of eastern North America; southern part of our region.

Nature Notes:

There are three North American *Nedra* species and others in the American tropics.

American Angle Shades *Euplexia benesimilis*

APRIL	MAY	JUNE	JULY	AUG	SEPT	OCT

Caterpillar Food: Alder, willows, viburnums, ferns, meadow rues & more

Nature Notes:

This moth might be a low-grade bird-dropping "mimic," but not as obviously so as in other species.

There are two North American species and the genus is sizable in the Old World.

Moth: Forewing brown with dark shading in basal and medial areas, a wide pale brown band outside the postmedial line and a conspicuous pale reniform spot.

Caterpillar: Usually deep green, sometimes brown, with a humped eighth segment marked by a pair of conspicuous white tubercles.

Life Cycle: Likely two generations. Pupa winters.

Range: Most of eastern U.S. and southern Canada, west in the north to Pacific and Alaska; our area to northern Ontario.

Olive Angle Shades *Phlogophora iris*

APRIL	MAY	JUNE	JULY	AUG	SEPT	OCT

Caterpillar Food: Apparently many herbaceous plants

Moth: Forewing rich olive green, fading to brown. Outer forewing with broad pale and narrower dark, lines. Outer margin strongly scalloped.

Caterpillar: Chunky, olive-green or pale brown, tapered in front, squared at rear, with a narrow, broken, pale dorsal line, vague dark oblique lines and a pale spiracular line.

Life Cycle: One generation in our area. Grown caterpillar winters.

Range: Northeastern U.S. across Canada to Saskatchewan; our area to northern Ontario.

Nature Notes:

Phlogophora means "flame bearer," for reasons unknown.

Phlogophora is a good-sized genus in the Old World, apparently represented in the Americas only by our two species.

Brown Angle Shades *Phlogophora periculosa*

APRIL	MAY	JUNE	JULY	AUG	SEPT	OCT

Caterpillar Food: Range of woody broadleaved and coniferous plants

Nature Notes:

The perching posture is quite remarkable, the forewings strongly rolled under along the costal area, producing an effect suggesting a curled dried leaf.

Moth: Forewings are brown with a variously darker **Y**-shaped median patch and a less deeply scalloped outer margin.

Caterpillar: Similar to that of Olive Angle Shades (*P. iris*), with a broken white dorsal line and a series of subdorsal white spots (see page 249).

Life Cycle: One generation in our area. Grown caterpillar winters.

Range: All across the northern U.S. and southern Canada; south through Appalachian Mountains to Georgia, Alabama.

Sharp Angle Shades *Conservula anodonta*

APRIL	MAY	JUNE	JULY	AUG	SEPT	OCT

Caterpillar Food: Unknown but I have reared on aspen and alder

Moth: Like a small Brown Angle Shades without a scalloped wing margin.

Caterpillar: Rich yellow green, with pale dorsal and subdorsal lines finely edged with black, many fine yellow lines; bright white subspiracular line runs down outside of hind prolegs. Head small, green.

Life Cycle: One generation. Pupa apparently winters.

Range: Northeastern U.S. and southern Canada; northern parts of our three-state region.

Nature Notes:

The light-captured female that laid eggs smelled bad in the container, suggesting the possibility of chemical defense. Resulting pupae eclosed in October, likely as an artifact of rearing conditions.

A small genus with one North American species and others in the tropics of Africa and Asia.

Columbine Borer Moth *Papaipema leucostigma*

APRIL	MAY	JUNE	JULY	AUG	SEPT	OCT

Caterpillar Food: Wild Columbine. Most species named for host plant

Nature Notes:

Because many species are specialists, quite a few are endangered by habitat destruction and degradation, especially those dependent upon prairie plants. Some are the rarest of the rare while, at the other extreme, a few generalists occasionally become pests on corn.

One species of interest to northern naturalists is *P. appassionata* which only feeds on Pitcher-Plants (*Sarracenia purpurea*) in bogs.

With at least 47 species, this is the largest noctuid genus restricted to North America. New species are still being found. A sampling of species is shown on the right hand page. Note that most are named after their host plant.

Moth: *Papaipema* adults are small to medium-sized, with forewings often yellow to orange, often boldly marked with clusters of white spots, but sometimes quite dark or drab gray-brown, with little or no marking. Wingspans from about 1 to 2 inches.

Caterpillar: Rarely seen due to burrowing habits within the stems, bulbs, roots or rhizomes of herbaceous plants. Their presence is variously signed by wilting, drooping, stunting, yellowing, browning or swellings, sometimes with frass pushed out through holes in stems.

Life Cycle: One generation in our area. Eggs dropped loose near host plants winter. Caterpillars mature and pupate in mid to late summer, inside or outside the host plant.

Range: Forty species of *Papaipema* occur in eastern North America, and at least 31 of these species can be found in our three-state region.

Other Borer Moths...

Burdock Borer
Papaipema cataphracta

Sensitive Fern Borer
Papaipema inquaesita

Bracken Borer
Papaipema pterisii

Culver's-root Borer
Papaipema sciata

Meadow-rue Borer
Papaipema unimoda

Ash Tip Borer
Papaipema furcata

Ironweed Borer
Papaipema cerussata

Stalk Borer
Papaipema nebris

Pitcher-Plant Borer
Papaipema appassionata

Cattail Borer
Bellura obliqua

Lost Sallow *Eupsilia devia*

APRIL	MAY	JUNE	JULY	AUG	SEPT	OCT

Caterpillar Food: Asters to oaks, but mostly broadleaved woody plants

Nature Notes:

Adults feed at early tree flowers such as maples and willows and also at sap flows.

Adults may fly on nights at or above freezing through the winter. During cold spells they likely hunker down under snow cover or leaf litter and let their temperatures go down "undefended;" that is, they do not warm up to survive. If they get too cold they die.

Moth: Brown to gray, often with a contrasting reniform spot. Identification is often a challenge, especially in spring. Lost Sallow is more distinct than most.

Caterpillar: Dark purplish with a broken white spiracular stripe and much paler below. Head shiny yellow with much dark across lower half. Hard to identify to species.

Life Cycle: One generation. Adult winters.

Range: Much of eastern U.S. and southern Canada; about six species in our southern area and one north to central Ontario.

Scalloped Sallow *Eucirroedia pampina*

APRIL	MAY	JUNE	JULY	AUG	SEPT	OCT

Caterpillar Food: Broadleaved plants; poplars, cherries, maples, oaks

Moth: Forewings yellow-orange, variably shaded with red-brown. Antemedial and post-medial lines yellow with red-brown shading. Orbicular and reniform spots filled with red-brown. All wings strongly scalloped.

Caterpillar: Variegated drab reddish brown, with vague, thin, white dorsal and subdorsal lines. Head darker. Warts pale with single dark hairs. Spiracles pale, dark-rimmed.

Life Cycle: One generation. Egg winters.

Range: Much of eastern U.S. and southern Canada; Nova Scotia to British Columbia.

Nature Notes:

Adults perch on leaf litter with heads pressed to the surface. When disturbed they scurry under leaf litter.

In a test with wild birds, these moths were readily eaten.

This is the only known *Eucirroedia* species.

Common Hyppa *Hyppa xylinoides*

APRIL	MAY	JUNE	JULY	AUG	SEPT	OCT

Caterpillar Food: A wide variety of herbaceous and low woody plants

Nature Notes:

The caterpillar is said to accumulate dew on its body, though how or to what end, seems unknown.

I found many small caterpillars on a single willow-herb plant, presumably resulting from clustered egg-laying. Ironically, there were numerous other plants of the same species nearby, so the behavior is enigmatic. I doubt they could all have been so laden with eggs.

Moth: Forewings brown, the strongest markings are basal and medial dashes near inner margin and white edging along the postmedial line, strongest near inner margin.

Caterpillar: Stout, variegated yellowish-brown to black, tapered at front, squared at rear. Broad pale spiracular stripe is narrowest on first thoracic segment.

Life Cycle: Two generations. Final-instar caterpillar or prepupa winters.

Range: Northern half of U.S. and southern Canada; Newfoundland to British Columbia.

Other Owlet Moths...

Variable Narrow-wing
Magusa divaricata

Yellow-striped Armyworm
Spodoptera ornithogalli

Chalcedony Midget
Elaphria chalcedonia

American Swordgrass
Xylena nupera

Dimorphic Pinion
Lithophane patefacta

American Bird's-wing
Dypterygia rozmani

Bicolored Sallow
Sunira bicolorago

Pink-banded Sallow
Xanthia tatago

Pale Enargia
Enargia decolor

Even-lined Sallow
Ipimorpha pleonectusa

American Dun-bar *Cosmia calami*

APRIL	MAY	JUNE	JULY	AUG	SEPT	OCT

Caterpillar Food: Oaks; but sometimes carnivorous on caterpillars

Nature Notes:

For unknown reasons the caterpillar's carnivory is highly variable. It has likely arisen in response to periodic defoliations when leaves are suddenly scarce but caterpillars abundant. Most other markedly carnivorous caterpillars, such as pinions, are found in early spring species.

A small holarctic genus with four North American species.

Moth: Forewings tan, variously shaded with brown, with distinct, slightly-curved antemedial line and strongly bent postmedial line, each pale with a dark edge.

Caterpillar: Stocky, pale green, with heavy speckling of pale irregular spots and a strong pale dorsal line.

Life Cycle: One generation. Egg winters.

Range: Much of U.S. except northern Great Plains and peninsular Florida; only very southern Canada from Nova Scotia to southern Saskatchewan.

Hitched Arches *Melanchra adjuncta*

APRIL	MAY	JUNE	JULY	AUG	SEPT	OCT

Caterpillar Food: Alder, willow, elm, goldenrod and many others

Moth: Forewing mottled with black and dark greenish brown, with strongly contrasting white zigzagging in basal area, along medial line and in subterminal area. Reniform spot large and white, with arching dark line within.

Caterpillar: Olive green, with dark olive semicircular marks on first and second abdominal segments; pair of olive triangles at rear.

Life Cycle: One (or two?) generations in our area. Pupa winters.

Range: Eastern U.S. to Pacific Northwest; Newfoundland to northern British Columbia.

Nature Notes:

Three other *Melanchra* species occur in North America, all in our area. All fly May or June into July or August. Some of the caterpillars are quite showy, suggesting they are chemically defended. Adults tend to be dark and poorly marked, some have distinctive white markings near the forewing anal angle.

Dingy Cutworm Moth *Feltia jaculifera*

APRIL	MAY	JUNE	JULY	AUG	SEPT	OCT

Caterpillar Food: Many plants; also crops such as alfalfa, flax, oats, wheat

Nature Notes:

This is very likely a cryptic complex of six or more species distinguishable only by chemical analysis.

Female *Feltia* species use their saberlike ovipositors to insert their eggs so deep inside flowers of the aster family that they are hard to detect.

There are 18 North American *Feltia* species.

Moth: Forewings dark, complexly and boldly marked with dingy white streaks. Orbicular and reniform spot also contrastingly pale. Difficult to distinguish from several other *Feltia* species by superficial appearance.

Caterpillar: Dull gray-brown, with dark shading forming wedge-shaped patches in center of each abdominal segment.

Life Cycle: One generation in our area. Winter as partly grown caterpillars.

Range: Nova Scotia to Alaska; south through most of U.S., including our area.

Flame-shouldered Dart *Ochropleura implecta*

APRIL	MAY	JUNE	JULY	AUG	SEPT	OCT

Caterpillar Food: Likely a variety of herbaceous and woody plants

Moth: Forewing reddish brown, with pale cream costa and strong black basal dash.

Caterpillar: Warm brown, tapered at front, squared at rear, with broken white dorsal and subdorsal lines and a broad pale spiracular line sharply bordered with white above. Spiracles dark rimmed.

Life Cycle: Likely two generations. Pupa winters.

Range: New England south to Alabama, Georgia; eastern Canada, Labrador west to British Columbia, Yukon.

Nature Notes:

Our species was only distinguished from the European *Ochropleura plecta* in 1998; many texts include the old name.

This is the only North American *Ochropleura* species with an unknown number in the Old World.

Great Brocade *Eurois occulta*

APRIL	MAY	JUNE	JULY	AUG	SEPT	OCT

Caterpillar Food: Esp. Tamarack; also poplar, willow, alder, blueberries

Nature Notes:

A female that I photographed was strongly inclined to drop to the ground and scurry under debris. There are other moths that drop and run rather than fly away.

There is speculation that population outbreaks of caterpillars may have contributed to the disappearance of Viking settlements in Greenland.

Some call it Great Gray Dart.

Moth: Forewings pale gray with brown shading; note large contrastingly pale orbicular spot and large pale curved reniform spot with darker shading within; black markings along outside of postmedial line and as a black dash in the median area.

Caterpillar: Stout, with subdorsal and spiracular series of dark wedge-shaped spots. Wide white spiracular band.

Life Cycle: One generation. Pupa winters.

Range: Holarctic, including northern U.S. and Canada; our area to treeline.

Great Brown Dart *Eurois astricta*

APRIL	MAY	JUNE	JULY	AUG	SEPT	OCT

Caterpillar Food: Aspen & other woody plants

Moth: Mostly dark brown (with a reddish shading in eastern part of range), lacking strong contrast, with large spots ringed in black. Somewhat paler in the median area. Lines zigzag but not highly conspicuous.

Caterpillar: Similar to that of Great Brocade, but with a violet cast and a larger head.

Life Cycle: One generation. Pupa likely winters.

Range: All across northern states north to treeline in central Canada and south in western mountains; all of our area.

Nature Notes:

Tends to be more common than Great Brocade.

Eggs of the Great Brocade and Great Brown Dart were laid (in captivity) in a large, many-layered, clump. Such arrangement may protect the inner eggs from tiny parasitoid wasps.

Microlepidoptera

This is a huge gathering of very diverse, not very closely related and poorly known moths in many different families, ranging from tiny (many) to large (a few), lumped for convenience. In North America there are about as many kinds of micromoths (6181 species) as macromoths (6242 species) known so far. Assuming that micromoths are easier to overlook, it is likely that micromoths outnumber macromoths. Thirty or more microlep families occur in our area. Though generally poorly known, some species of economic importance are among the very best studied of all moths. Space allows only the briefest glance at a few of the largest and most conspicuous families.

Ghost Moths Family Hepialidae

A family of small to large, very primitive moths. In many of our species congregated males signal pheromonally from expanded tibial scent brushes, while either flying or hanging from vegetation and fanning their wings, to attract females. Hovering evening mating swarms likely account for the family common name. They lack hearing organs and reduce exposure to bats by flying low and only for short periods of time or by calling from low perches. The taxonomy, including the extent of the family, remains substantially unresolved. Primitive Lepidoptera are not monophyletic. While the group encompasses just one percent of living moth species, it displays a great range of diversity, even including moths with jaws that chew pollen.

Moths

Can be quite large and showy for a member of the "microleps." Antennae are short and beaded. The wings are coupled by a finger-like projection called a jugum arising from the inner margin of the forewing near the base. Females lay large numbers of eggs, often strewing them near appropriate caterpillar food plants while in flight. These moths (especially the males, which fly the least) do not appear often at lights.

Caterpillars

Most caterpillars feed inside the stems and roots of trees, shrubs, ferns and grasses or externally on roots. Many or all early-instar caterpillars may be mycophagous (fungus feeding). Adults are cryptic in the typical perching posture, hanging limply by the extended front legs from vegetation.

Diversity (Species Richness/Range)

Over 500 species worldwide, including 19 in North America and about six in our area.

Silver-spotted Ghost Moth *Sthenopis argenteomaculatus*

11-0016

Four-spotted Ghost Moth *Sthenopis purpurascens*

11-0017

Willow Ghost Moth *Sthenopis thule*

11-0018

Plume Moths
Family Pterophoridae

Moths

Distinctive in their deeply notched outer wing margins and peculiar T-shaped perching posture in which the wings are held out perpendicular to the body, the hindwings folded within the forewings. In Latin America this has earned them the name "Jesus Christ moths." Adults lack tympanal hearing organs but have developed proboscі and males have been observed drinking at puddles. There is frenulum-retinaculum wing-coupling. Wingspans range from 0.5 to 1.6 inches.

Caterpillars

The caterpillars are commonly leaf tiers or borers in herbaceous plants. They are sparsely covered with clusters of conspicuous setae. The caterpillar of a southeastern U.S. species eats the sticky stalked glands of carnivorous sundew (*Drosera*) plants and the corpses of insects trapped there.

Diversity (Species Richness/Range)

A family of about 1000 species, with about 160 in North America. While relatively few species occur in our area (about 30 in all of Michigan) they are often seen.

Leafroller & Tortricid Moths Family Tortricidae

The family includes such famous and infamous species as the Mexican Jumping Bean Moth the Spruce Budworm Moth and the iconic worm inside apples, the Codling Moth.

Moths

Forewings are often squared off at the apex and many share a characteristic bell-shaped perching profile. The wings are coupled by a frenulum and retinaculum. They lack tympanal hearing organs. Mouthparts are well developed and most adults presumably feed. Wingspans 0.4 to 1.3 inches.

Caterpillars

Caterpillars feed inside shelters of silk-tied folded or rolled leaves, or bore inside roots, stems, fruits or seeds of their host plants.

Diversity (Species Richness/Range)

A large family of small to medium-sized moths, with over 6000 species worldwide and almost 1393 known, so far, in North America. Many species occur in our area (about 385 in all of Michigan) but most are poorly known.

Carpenterworm Moths
Family Cossidae

Moths

The wings are often gray or brown with markings in a reticulate (net-like) pattern. The abdomen extends well beyond the hindwings. The wings are coupled by a frenulum and retinaculum. There are no tympanal hearing organs. Adults do not feed but come to light. Antennae are simple (threadlike) in females and bipectinate (feathery) in males. Eggs are laid singly or in small groups in bark crevices. Wingspans 1.5 to 2.75 inches.

Caterpillars

Caterpillars feed inside living trees, especially, in our area, poplars and oaks, sometimes killing them. Since wood is a poor source of nitrogen (efficiency of conversion of food is nitrogen-dependent and can be as low as one percent in wood feeders), caterpillars require two to four years to gather enough nutrients to pupate.

Diversity (Species Richness/Range)

A group of over 700 small to large moths, with 46 species in North America and about five in our area.

Poplar Carpenterworm *Acossus centerensis*

Carpenterworm Moth *Prionoxystus robiniae*

Slug Caterpillar Moths Family Limacodidae

Moths

A family of small, mostly drab, chunky moths which do not feed and lack tympanal hearing organs. Wingspans range from 0.6 to 1.7 inches.

Caterpillars

The celebrities of this family are the caterpillars, a weird and wild menagerie of colors, shapes, patterns, textures and venoms. The prolegs are modified to a broad sucker-like pad and adhesion to the undersides of smooth leaves is aided by liquid silk. Their heads are largely hidden within the thorax, except for a ventral slit which allows them to feed.

The unmistakable Saddleback Caterpillar (*Acharia stimulea*) can only be found in our region in southern Lower Michigan. Many of the caterpillars in this family can deliver a nasty sting if their spines contact tender skin, and unusually sensitive persons could suffer serious consequences.

Diversity (Species Richness/ Range)

Over 1000 species worldwide, 49 in North America and 14 in our area.

Yellow-shouldered Slug Moth *Lithacodes fasciola*

Spiny Oak-slug Moth *Euclea delphinii*

Clearwing Moths Family Sesiidae

Some clearwing moths are so convincing in their resemblance to wasps, both in appearance and behavior, that this accounts partly for their infrequent collection.

Moths

The common family name refers to the usual scale-less transparent areas in the wings. Forewings are narrower than the hindwings. Sesiids have dual wing-coupling. In addition to a frenulum and retinaculum, the inner margin of the proximal forewing rolls under, coupling with a similarly up-rolled costal margin of the hindwing. Adults commonly feed at flowers, but only one species in our area comes at all to light. They are better sampled using simple traps baited with synthesized pheromones that lure the males. Some species have every-other-year patterns of occurrence. Wingspans from 0.6 to 1.25 inches.

Caterpillars

The caterpillars feed inside the stems and roots of many woody and herbaceous plants. One species can take a bite out of your zucchini patch, detectable by withered vines (though it might not reach our region—at least yet). Some specialize on boring into galls formed by other insects on willows or oaks.

Diversity (Species Richness/Range)

There are over 1000 species of these day-flying, small to medium-sized, wasp-mimic moths worldwide, with currently 135 in North America and about 25 in our area.

Maple Callus Borer *Synanthedon acerni*

Other Clearwing moths...

Virginia Creeper Clearwing
Albuna fraxini

Hornet Moth species
Sesia augeri

Squash Vine Borer
Melittia cucurbitae

Dogwood Borer
Synanthedon scitula

Riley's Clearwing
Synanthedon rileyana

Birch-borer Clearwing
Synanthedon fulvipes

Peachtree Borer
Synanthedon exitiosa

Ironweed Clearwing
Carmenta bassiformis

Window-winged Moths Family Thyrididae

Now members of the Superfamily Thyridoidea, but formerly part of Superfamily Pyraloidea.

Moths

Stout, chunky moths. Sometimes mistaken for butterflies since adults are often day-flying and will nectar at flowers. They have a unique perching posture in which their body is arched so their middle legs do not touch the substrate. Wings are held outstretched. Many have semi-transparent "windows" on their wings.

Spotted Thyris (below) is brownish and flecked with orange. Transluscent white spots and patches on wings. Multiple adults may gather at puddles, taking in fluids from wet soil. Mournful Thyris is black and dramatically spotted with white. Its pale wing patches are larger than on the Spotted Thyris.

Caterpillars

Concealed feeders that feast within a curled leaf. Some burrow in stalks and stems; even causing plant galls in some cases. Yellow body spotted with black; head is black.

Caterpillars of Spotted Thyris feed on *Clematis* and *Houstonia* species. *Clematis, Smilax* and grape host Mournful Thyris caterpillars.

Diversity (Species Richness/Range)

Primarily a tropical family with 760 species worldwide. Twelve North American species with three in our tri-state region. Spotted Thyris is slightly more northern in range than Mournful Thyris; found across the continent but sightings concentrated from New England to northern Georgia; scattered sightings across our region. Mournful Thyris mainly in southeastern U.S. with some sightings in southern parts of our three-state region.

Snout Moths
Family Pyralidae

A few species are important competitors with humans for food and fiber. The meal moth, *Pyralis farinalis*, is a common worldwide pest in stored food products; adults are sometimes found inside homes and can carry the rat tapeworm, which can infest humans. A small species (along with mosquitoes) pollinates the Blunt-leaf Orchid in Michigan.

The common family name refers to the usually long labial palps that project forward or upward. The scientific family name refers to "an insect fabled to live in fire." I do not know the story.

Moths

Adult pyralids have tympanal hearing organs located ventrally on the first abdominal segment and usually a well-developed proboscis that is scaled at the base and presumably used. They perch with the antennae folded back along the dorsal midline of the body. Wingspans range from 0.35 to 1.45 inches.

Caterpillars

Most of the caterpillars feed inside their food plants or in shelters created by tying folded or rolled leaves with silk. Some live as scavengers inside nests of bees or wasps. The sloth moths of tropical America are pyralids. Some sloths carry over 120 moths, which feed on sloth dung. Some species feed on aquatic plants in lakes and streams and have tracheal gills that allow them to breath underwater.

Diversity (Species Richness/Range)

This huge group of small to medium-sized moths is likely the most ecologically diverse family of Lepidoptera. There are about 25,000 named species, including 682 in North America. A large number remain unknown. While there are many species in our area (about 325 in all of Michigan), most are poorly known.

Meal Moth
Pyralis farinalis

Clover Hayworm
Hypsopygia costalis

Crambid Snout Moths
Family Crambidae

Moths

Includes the grass moths of subfamily Crambinae which perch inconspicuously on grasses with wings rolled around their body (see Double-banded Grass-veneer on facing page). Some with aquatic larva such as the *Paraponyx* of ponds and marshes. They can often be seen perching on lily pads during the day (see opposite page; four species in our region).

Caterpillars

Typically stem borers in grasses. The U.S. agricultural pest European Corn Borer (*Coniesta ignefusalis*) is a crambid introduced in early 1900s.

Diversity (Species Richness/Range)

Huge family with 10,347 species in over 1,000 genera worldwide. Range from drab to colorful. 864 species across North America.

Tropical Ermine Moths
Family Attevidae

Only one species in North America of this mostly tropical family. *Atteva aurea* (formerly *A. punctella*) was originally only found in the U.S. in south Florida, but the introduction of the Chinese Tree-of-Heaven to Philadelphia in 1784 changed everything. The tree spread naturally and via nursery sales until it reached Florida many decades later. The Ailanthus Webworm found it a very acceptable host and its population expanded north to now become quite abundant across eastern North America. Now found in southern halves of all three states with scattered northern records.

Moth

Day-flying and often found nectaring on flowers. Resembles a longhorn beetle when perched, and mimics a wasp in flight.

Caterpillar

As its common name implies, caterpillars live communally in a web. Hosts include the introduced *Ailanthus* Tree-of-Heaven. Some reports of caterpillars on sumacs.

Crambid Moths...

Glossary

Addorsal line: bilaterally paired visible line immediately to each side of the dorsal line.

Anal angle: angle near juncture of outer and inner margins of moth wing.

Anal plate: dorsal shield on the last abdominal segment of a caterpillar.

Anal prolegs: hindmost pair of prolegs of a caterpillar.

Antemedial line: a transverse line separating the basal and median areas of the forewing.

Anterior: front.

Apex: angle formed at the juncture of costal and outer margins of a moth wing.

Aposematism: use of signals (especially visual, sonic or odorant) to advertise toxicity, unpleasant taste, low nutritional value or other traits unfavorable to potential predators.

Basal area: area of forewing near attachment, bounded outwardly by antemedial line.

Cell (pupal): chamber burrowed or chewed into substrate (soil, wood, etc.) in which pupation occurs.

Cocoon: silk-bound shelter woven by a prepupal caterpillar prior to pupation; sometimes incorporates leaves, chewed wood, larval setae, etc.

Coremata: inflatable pheromone-releasing structures eversible from the abdomens of some male tiger moths.

Costa: front margin of a moth wing (costal margin).

Crepuscular: at dawn or dusk.

Cryptic: serving to avoid detection; also describes species so similar they are mistaken for one species.

Diapause: suspension of activity and development.

Dimorphic: having two different forms (e.g. sexual or seasonal).

Discal cell: a large cell near the wing base, widening distally.

Discal spot: a spot near the outer end of the discal cell; often more evident in the hindwing.

Disruptive coloration: a pattern of markings that obscure the true outline of an animal, making it harder for predators to detect.

Distal: away from the origin.

Dorsal: on top, versus ventral.

Eclosion: emergence from an egg or pupa.

Exuviae: the molted exoskeleton of an insect; larval or pupal in holometabolous insects.

Frass: material excavated by an internally feeding caterpillar; often used in reference to feculae.

Frenulum/retinaculum: wing-coupling mechanism involving single (males) or multiple (females) spines (frenulum) extending from the base of the hindwing and interlocking with a specialized tuft of scales along the underside of the forewing.

Hair pencil: tuft of long setae found in some caterpillars.

Hemolymph: the clear fluid filling the body cavities of an insect; similar to blood, but does not transport oxygen via specialized carrier cells.

Holarctic Region: combined temperate areas of the northern hemisphere; holarctic (adj.).

Instar: a larval stage between molts; typically five or six in Lepidoptera.

Labial palps: paired, sensory, scale-covered, upward-curved appendages that project forward from under the front of the head.

Lateral: to or on the side; away from the midline.

Latex: milky, often toxic, often abundantly-flowing, pressurized sap of some plants.

Melanism: a condition of unusually dark pigmentation; melanic (adj.).

Mesothorax: middle thoracic segment.

Mimicry: any of several sorts of resemblance of one organism (mimic) to one or more others (models), favored by the effect of the resemblance on one or more "third-party"(receiver, target) organisms; critically, the mimic and model are both organisms of interest to the receiver. This contrasts with similar resemblance relationships not involving three organisms (bird-dropping "mimicry") or in which the model is not of interest to the receiver (leaf /twig "mimicry").

Mullerian mimicry: mimicry in which more or less defended species improve protection from predators by adopting common appearances.

Nearctic Region: roughly, America north of Mexico; nearctic (adj.).

Parasite: a non-predatory organism that feeds upon another organism, not usually resulting in death of the host organism.

Parasitoid: an insect (usually a wasp or fly) whose larvae feed from within or upon the surface of the host egg, pupa, or caterpillar, usually resulting in death of the host organism (in this way more predator than parasite).

Parthenogenic: able to reproduce without mating or, if mating, without male genetic contribution.

Pheromone: a chemical released to the outside of an organism and acting on the same and/or other species.

Posterior: hind; at the rear; opposite of anterior.

Postmedial line: a transverse line separating the inner (median) and outer subterminal areas of the forewing and/or hind wing.

Prepupa: caterpillar that has ceased feeding, prior to pupation.

Proboscis: the tubelike, double, longitudinally-fused, usually coiled, sucking mouthpart of adult Lepidoptera.

Proleg: bilaterally paired, fleshy, unjointed, abdominal muscular appendage of a caterpillar.

Prothoracic shield: a dorsal plate over the first thoracic segment of a caterpillar.

Prothorax: front-most thoracic segment.

Pupa: stage of complete metamorphosis in which larval tissues are largely dissolved and reorganized into adult tissues.

Reniform spot: a kidney-shaped marking on the forewing near the costal margin.

Scale: a flattened seta; especially covering the wings of Lepidoptera in an overlapping arrangement.

Scent brush: eversible tuft of scales, especially on leg or abdomen of male Lepidoptera, used to disperse short-range mating pheromones.

Seta: a socketed, hair-like, outgrowth from the body wall (plural: setae).

Sexual dimorphism: showing distinct differences between the genders.

Silk: protein fiber secreted by glands of various sorts; in moth caterpillars, from modified salivary glands. Used in cocoons, as tether lines, as transport "balloons," in building various shelters and, in liquid form, as an adhesive in slug caterpillar moths (limacodids).

Spiracle: any of a series of lateral, valved openings through which invertebrates exchange oxygen and carbon dioxide via the branched, internal, tracheal network.

Stigma: silver-metallic markings in the median forewing of some plusiine noctuids.

Tegula: (plural: tegulae); bilaterally paired, epaulette-like appendage of the mesothorax, arising above and ahead of the forewing base and shielding it; usually covered with elongate scales.

Thorax: middle of three body sections of an insect, comprising three segments, each bearing true legs and/or wings; named (front to back) prothorax, mesothorax, metathorax.

Tracheal network: system of highly-branched tubules within the insect body that open at the spiracles and transport oxygen and carbon dioxide.

Tribe: a group of similar genera within a taxonomic family; name usually ending with the suffix –ini (e.g. Arctiini).

Tympanal hearing organ: a bilaterally paired hearing organ typically located on the metathorax or on the anterior abdomen (sometimes at the base of the wings) and tuned to ultrasound. Typically involve a membrane (tympanum, ear-drum) stretched over or within a cavity.

Ventral: on underside; opposite of dorsal.

Voucher: a labeled specimen and/or photograph collected to document the occurrence and features of an organism in a particular time and place.

Photo Credits

Amazingly, the vast majority of the photos were taken by the author. It is an outstanding body of work. We at Kollath-Stensaas filled in a few holes with images from the following talented photographers:

Parker Backstrom: 43 all, 93 (White Pine Angle), 94b, 111 Deep Yellow Euchlaena, 123i, 152bl, 173t, 188b, 190b, 197i, 232i, 253 Ironweed Borer, 254i, 255i, 257tr, Chalcedony Midget, Bicolored Sallow, 269t, 271 Squash Vine Borer, Riley's Clearwing, br, bl, 272 all

Stephen Cresswell: 35 all, 41b, 171b

Clinton Dexter-Nienhaus: 45b, 71b, 107t, 110br, 118b

t = top	r = right
b = bottom	l = left
i = inset	s = sidebar

Kyle Johnson: 111, 253 bl, 257 Dimorphic Pinion

Don Kaddatz: 60 all, 61 all

David Liebman: 10, 42b, 171t, i

Tom Murray: 86i, 156bl, 160b, 179 White-lined Snout caterpillar, 215bi

Andy Reago & Chrissy McClarren via Wikimedia Commons: 163bl, 257 American Bird's-wing, 273br

Mike Reese [www.wisconsin butterflies.org]: 12 venomous caterpillar, 38b

Allen Blake Sheldon: 77t, 152br

Sparky Stensaas [www.sparkyphotos.com]: 8tl, 9 White-lined Sphinx Moth, 14, 19t, 23t, i, 27i, 30i, 33 all, 40t, 42t, i, 44t, 50i, 51i, 55i, 59i, 62i, 63tr, 65t, 77b, 84 all, 85 all, 93tl, 95ir, il, 105i, 107 Purple Plagodis, 112i, 118t, i, 120tl, 124m, 125t, 127i, 128i, 129t, 135br, 139m, 146i, 153t, 154i, 155t, i, 157b, 158t, insets, 162 bottom inset, 163 top inset, m, mi, 164i, 168i, 177bri, 178i, 179 White-lined Snout, 193 Lunate Zale, 202t, 205b, 207mr, ml, br, bl, 215t, i, s, 219i, 220i, 233t, i, 234 all, 236i, 237b, 244i, 249t, i, 257 Yellow-striped Armyworm, American Swordgrass, br, bl, 259i, 260 all, 262i, 265m, 266 all, 267tl, br, bl, 268tr, tl, bl, 271tr, Dogwood Borer, 274, 275 all

Wikimedia Commons: 30bi (MeadowLore), 65i (Didier Descouens), 89i (Robert Aguilar; Smithsonian Environmental Research Center), 158b, 268br (Theresa Thom)

Ben Yokel: 45t

References, Sources & Websites

References

Beadle, David, and Seabrooke Leckie. 2012. *Peterson Guide to Moths of Northeastern North America.* Houghton Mifflin: Boston, New York.

Brown, S.G., G.H. Boettner and J.E. Yack. 2007. *Clicking caterpillars: acoustic aposematism in Antheraea polyphemus and other Bombycoidea.* Journal of Experimental Biology 210: 993-1005.

Conner, W.E. 2009. *Tiger Moths and Woolly Bears: Behavior, Ecology and Evolution of the Arctiidae.* Oxford University Press.

Cornell, H.V. and B.A. Hawkins. 1995. *Survival patterns and mortality sources of herbivorous insects: some demographic trends.* American Naturalist 145: 563-593.

Covell, Charles, V., Jr. 1984. *A Field Guide to the Moths of Eastern North America.* Houghton Mifflin: Boston. Reprinted 2005, Special Publication 12, Virginia Museum of Natural History. A valuable guide to over 1300 species (pinned specimens).

Ferge, Leslie A. and George J. Balogh. 2000. *Checklist of Wisconsin Moths (Superfamilies Drepanoidea, Geometroidea, Mimallonoidea, Bombycoidea, Sphingoidea and Noctuoidea).* Milwaukee Public Museum Contributions in Biology and Geology, Number 93. Of great use regionally.

Gentry, G.L. and L.A. Dyer. 2002. *On the conditional nature of neotropical caterpillar defenses against their natural enemies.* Ecology 83: 3108-3119.

Heinrich, Bernd. 1993. *The Hot-Blooded Insects: Strategies and Mechanisms of Thermoregulation.* Harvard University Press: Cambridge.

Himmelman, John. 2023. *Discovering Moths: Nighttime Jewels in Your Own Backyard, Eastern North American Species.* Stackpole Books: Lanham, MD.

Janzen, Daniel H. 1984. *Two ways to be a big moth: Santa Rosa saturniids and sphingids.* Oxford Surveys in Evolutionary Biology 1:85-140.

Lees, David, and Alberto Zilli. 2019. *Moths: A Complete Guide to Biology and Behavior.* Smithsonian Books: Washington, DC.

Marshall, Stephen. 2006. *Insects: their natural history and diversity.* Firefly Books. Amazing photo resource for identification of northeastern/boreal insects.

McGuffin, W.C. 1967-81. *Guide to the Geometridae of Canada (Lepidoptera).* Memoirs of the Entomological Society of Canada 50 (Parts 1-4).

Pohl, G.R., Patterson, B., & Pelham, J.P. 2016. *Annotated taxonomic checklist of the Lepidoptera of North America, North of Mexico.* Working paper published online by the authors at ResearchGate.net. 766 pp. Known as "P3."

Riotte, J.C.E. 1992. *Annotated List of Ontario Lepidoptera.* Royal Ontario Museum Miscl Publications. Toronto. Great source for northern part of our area.

Sargent, T.D. 1976. *Legion of Night: The Underwing Moths.* University of Massachusetts Press: Amherst, MA.

Sargent, T.D. 1995. *On the relative acceptabilities [sic] of local butterflies and moths to local birds.* Journal of the Lepidopterists' Society 49(2): 148-162.

Scoble, M.J. 1992. *The Lepidoptera: Form, Function and Diversity.* Oxford University Press.

Sourakov, Andrei, and Rachel Warren Chadd. 2022. *The Lives of Moths: A Natural History of our Planet's Moth Life*. Princeton University Press: Princeton, NJ.

Stehr, F.W. (editor) 1987. *Immature Insects. Volume I.* Kendall/Hunt Publishing Co., Dubuque, IA.

Tuskes, P.M., J.P. Tuttle and M.M. Collins. 1996. *The Wild Silk Moths of the United States and Canada*. Cornell University Press. Ithaca, N.Y.

Tuttle, J.P. 2007. *The Hawk Moths of North America: A Natural History Study of the Sphingidae of the United States and Canada.* Wedge Entomological Foundation.

Wagner, D.L. 2005. *Caterpillars of Eastern North America*. Princeton University Press: Princeton, NJ. An excellent guide to nearly 700 species.

Winter, W.D. 2000. *Basic Techniques for Observing and Studying Moths and Butterflies*. Memoirs of the Lepidopterists' Society Number 5. Natural History Museum. Los Angeles, CA.

Wright, Amy Bartlett. 1993. *Peterson First Guides: Caterpillars*. Houghton Mifflin: Boston, New York. A great starter guide.

Sources

There has been a gap in sources for moth nets, collecting and storage equipment since BioQuip went out of business. Ecology Supplies has started to fill that niche: ecologysupplies.com.

Great Lakes IPM (Integrated Pest Management) greatlakesipm.com is a good place to purchase traps and pheromone lures for clearwing moths.

Websites

Bug Guide bugguide.net. Identification of your insect and spider photos. Thousands of species covered with input from enthusiasts and experts.

Butterflies and Moths of North America butterfliesandmoths.org is especially useful for including life history and ID tips for many species.

iNaturalist inaturalist.org has become *the* place for folks to post all their sightings with photos. Be aware that identification is crowd-sourced. There are also Projects for all three states; search "Michigan moths," etc. Invaluable world maps!

The Lepidopterists' Society lepsoc.org is a great source in many ways, including annual Season Summary report.

North American Moth Photographers Group mothphotographersgroup.msstate.edu is an excellent site for photographs of pinned and live moths and some caterpillars. Maps can be enlarged to show phenology for each state.

Toronto Entomologists' Association ontarioinsects.org. Great source of info on Ontario leps, including a very detailed moth atlas and annual season summaries.

University of Alberta has great info on many species included in this guide search.museums.ualberta.ca.

Moths of the Pacific Northwest is another go-to for species that range East-West and especially northern species https://pnwmoths.biol.wwu.edu/

Other useful sites: https://www.sphingidae.us/, https://www.thecaterpillarlab.org/

Caterpillar Food Plants

alders (*Alnus* spp.)
ashes (*Fraxinus* spp.)
aspens (*Populus* spp.)
asters (*Aster* spp.)
Basswood (*Tilia americana*)
Beaked Hazel (*Corylus cornuta*)
bedstraws (*Galium* spp.)
bergamots (*Monarda* spp.)
Black Cherry (*Prunus serotina*)
Black Locust (*Robinia pseudoacacia*)
Blue Beech (*Carpinus caroliniana*)
blueberries (*Vaccinium* spp.)
Bog Buckbean (*Menyanthes trifolium*)
Bog Rosemary (*Andromeda glaucophylla*)
Box Elder (*Acer negundo*)
Bracken Fern (*Pteridium aquilinum*)
Bur Oak (*Quercus macrocarpa*)
bur-reeds (*Sparganium* spp.)
burdocks (*Arctium* spp.)
bush-clovers (*Lespedeza* spp.)
cherries (*Prunus* spp.)
chickweeds (*Cerastium* spp.)
clematis (*Clematis* spp.)
clovers (*Trifolium* spp.)
cranberries (*Vaccinium* spp.)
Creeping Snowberry (*Gaultheria hispidula*)
currants (*Ribes* spp.)
Dandelion (*Taraxacum officinale*)
docks (*Rumex* spp.)
dogbanes (*Apocynum* spp.)
dogwoods (*Cornus* spp.)
Eastern Hemlock (*Tsuga canadensis*)
elderberries (*Sambucus* spp.)
elms (*Ulmus* spp.)
evening primroses (*Oenothera* spp.)
Fireweed (*Epilobium angustifolium*)
firs (*Abies* spp.)
goldenrods (*Solidago* spp.)
gooseberries (*Ribes* spp.)
grapes (*Vitis* spp.)
greenbriers (*Smilax* spp.)
Hackberry (*Celtis occidentalis*)
hawthorns (*Crataegus* spp.)
hazels (*Corylus* spp.)
Hemlock (*Tsuga canadensis*)
honeysuckle (*Lonicera* spp.)
Hop Hornbeam (*Ostrya virginiana*)
Hops (*Humulus lupulus*)
irises (*Iris* spp.)
ironweed (*Vernonia* spp.)
Ironwood (*Ostrya virginiana*)
Jack Pine (*Pinus banksiana*)
jewelweeds (*Impatiens* spp.)
joe-pye-weed (*Eutrochium* spp.)
juneberries (*Amelanchier* spp.)
Lilac (*Syringa vulgaris*)
Lowbush Blueberry (*Vaccinium angustifolium*)
lupines (*Lupinus* spp.)
meadow-rues (*Thalictrum* spp.)
meadowsweet (*Spiraea alba*)
milkweeds (*Asclepias* spp.)
mints (*Menthis* spp.)
Moonseed (*Menispermum canadense*)
Nannyberry (*Viburnum lentago*)
N. White Cedar (*Thuja occidentalis*)
oaks (*Quercus* spp.)
phloxes (*Phlox* spp.)
Pin Cherry (*Prunus pensylvanica*)
pines (*Pinus* spp.)
poison ivy (*Toxicodendron* spp.)
poplars (*Populus* spp.)
Purple Loosestrife (*Lythrum salicaria*)
Quaking Aspen (*Populus tremuloides*)
ragweeds (*Ambrosia* spp.)
ragworts (*Senecio* and *Packera* spp.)
Red Elderberry (*Sambucus racemosa*)
Red Maple (*Acer rubrum*)
Red Pine (*Pinus resinosa*)
Red-berried Elder (*Sambucus racemosa*)
Reed Canary Grass (*Phalaris arundinacea*)
sedges (*Carex* spp.)
Sensitive Fern (*Onoclea sensibilis*)
Silver Maple (*Acer saccharinum*)
smartweeds (*Polygonum* spp.)
snowberries (*Symphoricarpos* spp.)
St. Johnsworts (*Hypericum* spp.)
Stinging Nettle (*Urtica dioica*)
Sugar Maple (*Acer saccharum*)
sumacs (*Rhus* spp.)
sunflowers (*Helianthus* spp.)
Sweet Fern (*Comptonia peregrina*)
Sweet Gale (*Myrica gale*)
Tall Meadow-rue (*Thalictrum dasycarpus*)
Tamarack (*Larix canadensis*)
thistles (*Cirsium* spp.)
touch-me-nots (*Impatiens* spp.)
Tuliptree (*Liriodendron tulipifera*)
viburnums (*Viburnum* spp.)
violets (*Viola* spp.)
virgin's bowers (*Clematis* spp.)
Virginia Creeper (*Parthenocissus quinquefolia*)
walnuts (*Juglans* spp.)
White Meadowsweet (*Spiraea alba*)
White Spruce (*Picea glauca*)
Wild Columbine (*Aquilegia canadensis*)
wild plums (*Prunus* spp.)
willowherbs (*Epilobium* spp.)
willows (*Salix* spp.)
Winterberry (*Ilex verticillata*)
Wood Nettle (*Laportea canadensis*)
wood-sorrels (*Oxalis* spp.)
woodbines (*Parthenocissus* spp.)

Index

Quick Moth Finder

More of our user-friendly field guides

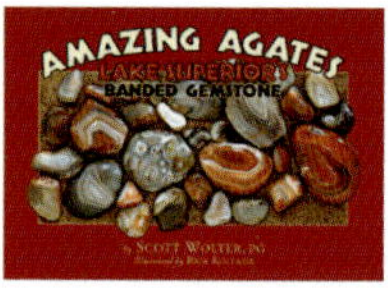

Amazing Agates

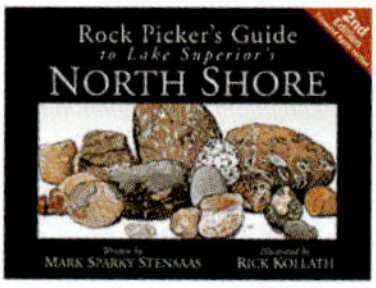

Rock Picker's Guide

Wildflowers of the BWCA

Fascinating Fungi of the North Woods
Cora Mollen & Larry Weber

Orchids of the North Woods
Kim & Cindy Risen

Amphibians & Reptiles MN, WI, MI
Allen Blake Sheldon

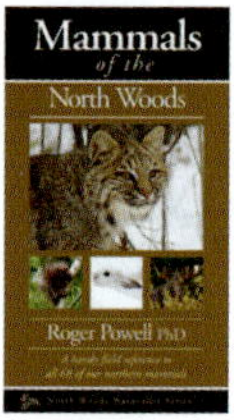

Mammals of the North Woods
Roger/Consie Powell

Damselflies of MN, WI & MI
Robert DuBois

Tiger Beetles Of MN, WI & MI
Mathew Brust

Butterflies of the North Woods
Larry Weber

Dragonflies of the North Woods
Kurt Mead

Ferns of the North Woods
Joe Walewski

Lichens of the North Woods
Joe Walewski

Spiders of the North Woods
Larry Weber

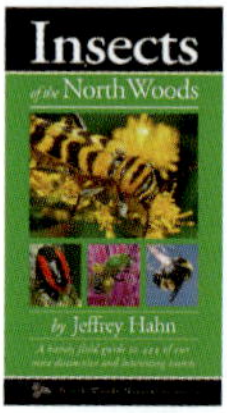

Insects of the North Woods
Jeff Hahn